DRESSING GOD

DRESSING GOD

by
GARRY HARRIS

WORD & SPIRIT
PUBLISHING

Unless otherwise indicated all scripture quotations are taken from the AMPC Amplified® Bible, Copyright © 1954, 1958, 1962, 1964, 1965, 1987 by The Lockman Foundation Used by permission. www.lockman.org

Scripture quotations marked MSG are taken from The Message, copyright © by Eugene H. Peterson, 1993, 1994, 1995, 1996. Used by permission of NavPress Publishing Group.

Scripture quotations marked NASB are taken from the New American Standard Bible®, Copyright © 1960, 1962, 1963, 1968, 1971, 1972, 1973, 1975, 1977, 1995 by The Lockman Foundation. Used by permission.

Dressing God
Copyright © 2025 by Garry Harris
ISBN: 978-1-685730-79-6

Published by Word and Spirit Publishing
P.O. Box 701403
Tulsa, Oklahoma 74170
wordandspiritpublishing.com

Printed in the United States of America. All rights reserved under International Copyright Law. Content and/or cover may not be reproduced in whole or in part in any form without the expressed written consent of the Publisher.

The purpose of this book is to

"stimulate and promote the faith of God's chosen ones and to lead them on to accurate discernment and recognition of and acquaintance with the Truth which belongs to and harmonizes with and tends to godliness,
[resting] in the hope of eternal life, [life] which the ever-truthful God Who cannot deceive promised before the world or the ages of time began."

—Titus 1:1-2

Contents

FOREWORD ix
INTRODUCTION xi
CHAPTER 1 – AGE OF DECEPTION 1
CHAPTER 2 – THE NAKED CHURCH 9
CHAPTER 3 – THE BLESSINGS OF OBEDIENCE 19
CHAPTER 4 – IS CLOTHING OPTIONAL? 23
CHAPTER 5 – WE SERVE A GOD WHO IS TO BE FEARED 39
CHAPTER 6 – THE GREATEST OBSTACLE TO HOLINESS 49
CHAPTER 7 – DEFINING DEVIANCY DOWNWARD 65
CHAPTER 8 – WHAT'S IN A NAME? SOMETIMES EVERYTHING 73
CHAPTER 9 – WHAT'S AT STAKE? ETERNITY 83
CHAPTER 10 – WHAT'S AT STAKE? (PART 2) – HEAVEN 87
CHAPTER 11 – WHAT'S AT STAKE? (PART 3) – HELL 95
CHAPTER 12 – REPENTANCE 111
CHAPTER 13 – ARE YOU READY TO MAKE A DECISION 121
CHAPTER 14 – ETERNAL SECURITY? 125
CHAPTER 15 – THE IMPORTANCE OF PROPHECY 139
CHAPTER 16 – OUR INHERITANCE AND REWARDS 149
CHAPTER 17 – THE MARRIAGE SUPPER OF THE LAMB 157
CHAPTER 18 – UNSPEAKABLE JOY AND FULL OF GLORY 167
CHAPTER 19 – THE REST OF THE STORY 171
EPILOGUE 183
ENDNOTES 185

Foreword

I have read that on average only 30 percent of people who purchase books actually finish reading them. Recently, I read a book recommended by a sister in Christ who has had a tremendous influence on my wife and me. Some books from the very start are referred to as page-turners—so captivating that it keeps you wanting to read more. The book she recommended was not that kind of book for me. It was a good book, but at times I struggled to keep reading it. But because it came highly recommended by someone I respected, I plowed on.

As a result of reading that book, I had an epiphany. I was nearing the end of the book and suddenly there were two pages that changed everything. I was in the basement of our home and had just finished reading those two pages when my wife called for me to come up for breakfast. In essence, it was a summation of everything from the beginning that made all that I had previously read crystal clear. As I was heading upstairs, I was giddy with thanksgiving that I hadn't stopped reading it.

I love reading, so there aren't many books in my library that I haven't finished. Most of the books I purchase are recommendations from pastors, friends, or authors I am familiar with. That, I believe, is what makes the difference for me. On the other hand, the chance that you are reading this and have actually heard of me is practically slim to none—and slim has already left town. You may have purchased this book because the picture on the cover attracted your attention or because of the unique title. Or, maybe you read the back cover and you purchased this book because the Holy Spirit has been tugging at your heart to become more like Jesus.

My whole purpose in writing this foreword is because of the first line above. I would love to author a real page-turner, but I'm not under any illusion that this book is one of those. This is actually a serious book about eternal matters. I hope there will be chapters that you love and that you learn new truths that you will find exciting. But I also realize there may be a chapter, like Chapter 14, that may actually make you angry because it's contrary to what you've been taught and believe. You might even think this author is clueless—or you might just lose interest. As a result you may be one of the 70 percent that doesn't finish the book.

When I think about the many different titles and authors in my library, for the most part it is true that there were only one or two passages that stuck with me in any given book. Now it could be that it's because my memory is like my hair—it doesn't stay with me. But I don't think I'm that much different from everyone else. That's why I highlight passages in all my books to aid me in finding those special truths to share with others.

I have dreamed of writing a book since my early twenties, but I didn't want to write a book just so I could claim to be an author. I am convinced that God called me to write this book. In light of that fact, I believe there is something included for everyone. Because I truly believe that, I'm asking you if, for whatever reason, you start losing interest, to just move on to the next chapter. My prayer is when you finish this book there will be at least one thing that will cause you to say: "that was money well spent."

—The Author

INTRODUCTION

"There is no greater mockery of the church than a life that claims Christ and yet is unchanged by him."

—ANONYMOUS

*N*ow you may be asking, "What kind of title is *Dressing God* for a book? Does God, the One Who created everything, this world on which we live with all its beauty and wonder, the universe in all its splendor and glory, need our help in dressing Himself?" Your answer would probably be, "Of course He doesn't."

As a matter of fact, I had another title in mind, but I wasn't happy with it. While in prayer, the Holy Spirit spoke to me about what it should be. My first thought on the title was, "That really sounds sacrilegious." This is coming from a guy who went into work one day and one of my female co-workers said when seeing me, "Your wife didn't see you when you left for work, did she? Cause I know if she saw you dressed like that she wouldn't have let you out of the house."

I'm sure that there's not one of us who would want the responsibility of dressing God. Could you imagine being responsible for the way He looks to all His creation?

And yet the Bible says we all are responsible to do just that. Now, you may be saying, "I'm going to have to see the chapter and verse in regard to that statement." Okay, here it is: "For you have been bought for a price: therefore glorify God in your body" (1 Corinthians 6:20 NASB).

In *Thayer's Greek Lexicon*, the fourth definition of the word glory is: By a use not found in secular writings **to make glorious, adorn with lustre, clothe with splendor.**[1] Hence the title *Dressing God*. We are to clothe God with honor (glory), by the way we live our lives.

The first mention of clothing in the Bible was after Adam and Eve sinned in the Garden of Eden. They were afraid and hid themselves from God because they were naked. The Bible tells us, "And the LORD God made garments of skin for Adam and his wife, and clothed them" (Genesis 3:21 NASB). In order to cover their nakedness and remove their shame, an animal had to die.

Death did not enter the world until man sinned. Do you realize that the first living thing that died was killed by the very One who created it? In the New Testament, Jesus is referred to as the Author of life (Acts 3:15), but man's sin caused Jesus to become the Author of death. Imagine how much it grieved Jesus Christ to kill the very thing He gave life to in order to cover man's shame.

And how did mankind repay Him? It was because of our sin that Jesus was stripped of His clothing when He was crucified in our place, because the penalty for sin was death. He experienced the righteous judgment of death for our sake so that we could live. He suffered the

INTRODUCTION

humiliation of the cross so that we might be clothed in His righteousness. The sins we commit as Christians clothe Him with shame in the eyes of the world.

WE ARE AMBASSADORS

In John Chapter 17, the Apostle John records what has been referred to as Jesus' high priestly prayer. In verses 10b-11a (MSG) Jesus said, "my life is on display in them, for I'm no longer going to be visible in the world ..." As the blood-bought church, God has called us to be His representatives to the lost people of this world. God has given us a mandate and He expects us to fulfill it. We know it as the Great Commission: "Go, therefore, and make disciples of all the nations ... teaching them to obey everything I have commanded you" (Matthew 28:19-20 NASB), so "Therefore, we are ambassadors for Christ, as though God were making an appeal through us; we beg you on behalf of Christ, be reconciled to God" (2 Corinthians 5:20 NASB).

Here is the definition of an ambassador: "Ambassadors are the highest-ranking diplomats of the U.S. and are usually based at the embassy in the host country ... ambassadors serve 'at the pleasure of the President,' meaning they can be dismissed at any time."[2] As Christ's highest-ranking representatives to a lost world, we have a responsibility to live our lives in a way that brings glory and honor to His name. So, the way we clothe Christ is by the way we live. If we walk in obedience to Him, then we clothe Him with glory and honor.

Today's Church has many enemies, but it's my contention that one of the greatest enemies doing the most harm to the person and the message of Jesus Christ, second only to Satan himself, are those who call themselves Christians. You may have heard Mahatma Gandhi's famous quote about Christians. He said, "I like your Christ, I do not like your Christians. Your Christians are so unlike your Christ."

NAKED SAINTS

In Revelation 3, Jesus, speaking through the Apostle John to the last of the seven churches, Laodicea, has this to say about them: "I know your [record of] works *and* what you are doing; you are neither cold nor hot. Would that you were cold or hot! So, because you are lukewarm and neither cold nor hot, I will spew you out of My mouth! For you say, I am rich; I have prospered *and* grown wealthy, and I am in need of nothing; and you do not realize *and* understand that you are wretched, pitiable, poor, blind, and naked" (Revelation 3:15-18).

So, the question you need to honestly answer as Christ's representative here on earth is this: "Are you clothing Him with glory, honor, and splendor; or are you making Him appear as a pitiful, blind beggar, threadbare and homeless?" My hope is that this book will become medicine for your eyes so you can see—really see.

TAILORS FOR GOD

In my opinion one of the most important questions a devoted follower of Christ needs to have answered is, "What is God's will for my life?" There is His general will (for every believer), and then there is His specific will (for the individual).

I believe God's general will for every believer, starting with me, is to be His tailor. Let me say up front that I'm not a tailor by trade, nor am I the son of a tailor. As I wrote that sentence it felt like the Holy

INTRODUCTION

Spirit shouted, "Whoa, hold on a second! Actually, you are the son of a tailor."

It then dawned on me that when we were born again we became children of God (John 1:12), and He has clothed us in His righteousness. He has made garments of salvation for us. At the Marriage Supper of the Lamb, He provides us with wedding garments: "The Marriage of the Lamb has come; his Wife has made herself ready. She was given a bridal gown of bright and shining linen. The linen is the righteousness of the saints" (Revelation 19:7-8 MSG).

Wow, God is our tailor! Just imagine how awesome the clothes He gives us are! We're going to have a closet that is full because of Him. We will be shouting with Isaiah: "I will sing for joy in God, explode in praise from deep in my soul! He dressed me up in a suit of salvation, he outfitted me in a robe of righteousness, as a bridegroom who puts on a tuxedo and a bride a jeweled tiara" (Isaiah 61:10-11 MSG).

There is a story in John about Jesus healing a blind man. "And His disciples asked Him, 'Rabbi, who sinned, this man or his parents, that he would be born blind?' Jesus answered, 'It was neither that this man sinned, nor his parents; but it was so that the works of God might be displayed in him'" (John 9:2-3 NASB). It then says that He bent down, spat in the dirt, and made some mud, placing it on the blind man's eyes. Jesus told him go wash in the Pool of Siloam and the man came home seeing.

Colossians Chapter 1 tells us that Jesus is the visible image of the invisible God. Jesus told Philip "The one who has seen Me has seen the Father" (John 14:9 NASB). We are the visible image of the invisible Jesus. Jesus has sent us into this world so that His glory may be displayed in us.

DRESSING GOD

God is very particular on how we represent Him to the world. He has made His Word available to us and that it is all that we need to learn how to become master tailors. What follows is my attempt to help you become our Master's tailor. Here's to having holy mud in your eyes!

CHAPTER 1

AGE OF DECEPTION

Satan has a template for every deception:
"Did God really say . . . ?"

*E*verything in this book is based on what the Bible says. Because of that, if it is to have any possibility of making an impact on the reader, the reader must first decide in their own mind the credibility of the Bible. Many who will read this have already concluded that the Bible is the inerrant, infallible, Word of God; this means that it is free from error or mistakes.

The Bible itself declares this to be true in 2 Timothy 3:16-17: "Every Scripture is God-breathed (given by His inspiration) and profitable for instruction, for reproof *and* conviction of sin, for correction of error *and* discipline in obedience, [and] for training in righteousness (in holy living, in conformity to God's will in thought, purpose, and action), so that the man of God may be complete *and* proficient, well fitted *and* thoroughly equipped for every good work."

However, there are others who sincerely want to believe but aren't convinced. Socrates thought that we should question absolutely everything. That statement sounds like it came right out of Satan's playbook.

In the beginning Satan created a template for every temptation. He needed only four words: "Did God really say . . . ?" All he has to do is fill in the blank when these thoughts appear in our minds. Here are just a few examples of how he tempts us to disobey God:

Did God really say . . . that divorce was a sin, and that He hated it? God loves you! He would want you to be happy. (Malachi 2:16; Matthew 19:3-4,9)

Did God really say . . . that you should always tell the truth? If you are a pastor reading this, who's had a moral failure and told the truth, you could possibly destroy the faith of hundreds, if not thousands, of people. Surely God wouldn't want that? (Proverbs 12:22; Ephesians 4:15; John 8:44)

Did God really say . . . that homosexuality is sinful? He's the one who created you, at least that's what the Bible says, and if He created you then that means He gave you those desires. (Genesis 18:20; Leviticus 18:22–20:13; Judges chapters 19-21; Romans 1:21-28)

Did God really say . . . that there is a hell and all who do not believe in him will go there to suffer for all eternity? How could a God of love be so cruel? That's not the God I know. (Matthew 25:46; Mark 9:43–48; Luke 16:23–24; Revelation 14:11)

Did God really say . . . that if anyone would follow him, he must deny himself, and take up his cross to do so? You've got to be kidding me! If you do that it will cause you to be depressed, anxious, and unsure of yourself. Not only that but you will never have any fun. (Matthew 16:24; Luke 9:23-25)

FALSE TEACHERS

Satan now uses professors of Religious Studies in secular universities, and sad to say, in Christian Seminaries as well, who try to dispossess those of us with their scholarly arguments who are foolish enough to believe all that the Bible says. According to them, ours is a blind faith. Those more enlightened, more educated individuals believe that faith unexamined is akin to self-delusion. People like these learned professors must challenge our faith by asking us, "did God really say that?"

For those of you who have doubts and would like to have answers to your questions about the Bible, I would highly recommend books on apologetics, which is a branch of theology devoted to the defense of the divine origin and authority of Christianity. Two of my favorites are *Evidence That Demands A Verdict* by Josh McDowell (Campus Crusade for Christ, 1972), and *I Don't Have Enough Faith to Be An Atheist* by Norm Geisler and Frank Turek (Crossway Books, 2004).

DAYS OF DECEPTION

Now you have more than likely heard the old saying, "If something seems too good to be true, it probably is too good to be true." In an article originally published in *The New York Times* on December 19, 2023, Emma Dibdin writes, "The past decade has seen an alarming surge in scams across the world, as digital life has created a whole new playbook for criminals to prey on the vulnerable. Combined with a political and cultural climate in which lies, disinformation and outright fraud seem to run rampant (just consider high-profile examples like Elizabeth Holmes and Sam Bankman-Fried), it's easy to feel surrounded by grifters."[3]

The last days before the coming of Christ will be a time of great deception. In Matthew 24:4, Jesus speaks of the last days by saying, "Take heed that no man deceive you." The apostle Paul speaks of a great apostasy (falling away) that will take place before the man of lawlessness is revealed by saying, "The coming [of the lawless one, the antichrist] is through the activity *and* working of Satan and will be attended by great power and with all sorts of [pretended] miracles and signs *and* delusive marvels—[all of them] lying wonders—and by unlimited seduction to evil *and* with all wicked deception for those who are perishing (going to perdition) because they did not welcome the Truth *but* refused to love it that they might be saved" (2 Thessalonians 2:9-10).

In yet another letter to Timothy, Paul writes, "But the [Holy] Spirit distinctly *and* expressly declares that in latter times some will turn away from the faith, giving attention to deluding *and* seducing spirits and doctrines that demons teach . . ." (1 Timothy 4:1).

And now we have the specter of AI impersonation because they now have an Open AI Voice Engine Software that can mimic human voices. Combine that with the very convincing videos of famous personalities or official government representatives that appear to be saying things they never actually said, and you have deception happening on a massive scale.

The above-mentioned passages on deception in the Bible, written nearly 2000 years ago, are clearly displayed in the headlines of print and electronic media news sources today. This is one of the many proofs that show that we are living in the last days before the coming of Christ.

You've all heard of fake news in regard to news outlets that have politically leaning agendas. They report on what they want you to hear and suppress any news that is contrary to their storyline.

Now, combine that with educational institutions from grades K-12, as well as universities, who are indoctrinating our children by teaching revisionist history and promoting anti-biblical truth by teaching evolution and situational ethics; this creates a public and a church that is biblically illiterate and ripe for deception. Their underlying teaching is "All truth is relevant to culture and to your experience. What is true for you isn't necessarily true for me." In other words, there are no moral absolutes.

As I write this, in the past few months there have been many reports of pastors and teachers admitting to moral failures and even criminal acts. This adds to Matthew 24:24 where Jesus says there will be many false Christs and prophets in the last days. Satan's goal is to have us question whether we can trust anything coming from the pulpit. As Hannah Arendt (German historian and philosopher – 1906-1975), said so insightfully: "This constant lying is not aimed at making people believe a lie, but at ensuring that no one believes anything anymore." If you want to know how bad it will become, please read all of Matthew 23 and 2 Peter 2.

TECHNOLOGY

This is possibly the greatest and most dangerous deception of all for Christians. Israeli historian Yuval Noah Harari, said in a news report on CNE News when questioned about artificial intelligence that "we are almost like gods. We have the power to create new life forms and destroy much of life on earth, including ourselves. . . . AI, says Harari, is different from all other technologies because it can make decisions by itself." He went on to say something that sent shock waves through the Christian community. He compared the development of AI with that of the printing press. "'The Gutenberg printing press printed as many Bibles as it was ordered to do. But it could not write a "single new page.' However, Harari said, 'AI can do that. It can even write a new Bible . . . In a few years, there may be religions that are actually correct,' he said with a smirk."[4]

How many Christians use electronic devices to read the Bible? And how many Christians will be easily led astray because they don't know the Bible well nor recognize when scripture has been changed to suit new cultural norms?

As you can see, we as a society are ripe for deception. Satan is creating a perfect storm of confusion, unrest, and instability in the last days while God uses him to fulfill the prophecies of the Bible that warns us of these things. It reminds me of what Martin Luther once said, "Even the devil is God's devil." Don't you know that really fries Satan's bacon? God uses him to fulfill His purposes and Satan can't do a single solitary thing about it.

One of my favorite podcasts is Olive Tree Ministries with Jan Markell. She has a saying which I really like: "Things aren't falling apart; they are falling into place."

PROPHECIES AND THE LAST DAYS

There are at least 300 prophecies in the Old Testament that concern Jesus' first coming. Every one of them came true. Peter Stoner in *Science Speaks* (Moody Press, 1963) shows that coincidence is ruled out by the science of probability. "Stoner says that by using the modern science of probability in reference to [just] eight prophecies, (concerning Jesus), we find that the chance that any man might have lived down to the present time and fulfilled all eight prophecies is 1 in 10 to the 17th power. That would be 1 in 100,000,000,000,000,000."[5] The fulfillment of prophecy is further proof of the authenticity and reliability of the Bible.

ARE YOU TRULY READY?

There are many who think it's a foregone conclusion that they are going to heaven when they die. If that's the case, why did Jesus say, "Don't look for shortcuts to God. The market is flooded with surefire, easygoing formulas for a successful life that can be practiced in your spare time. Don't fall for that stuff, even though crowds of people do. The way to life—to God!—is vigorous and requires total attention" (Matthew 7:13-14 MSG).

As I said previously, there are many in the church today who think they've got it made when their time comes to enter eternity. They've made a confession of faith—they believe they're set. God is truly a God of love, mercy, and grace, but He is also a holy God and a God of justice.

I would like to try and remove any thought the reader may have, specifically, that they can put their life in Christ on cruise control and waltz through the pearly gates of heaven when their time comes. "The

Lord saw that the wickedness of man was great in the earth, and that every imagination and intention of all human thinking was only evil continually" (Genesis 6:5 NASB). As a result, He brought judgment upon the world through the Flood.

On the answersingenesis.org website, I found this about the earth's pre-flood population. "If the growth rate in the pre-Flood world was equal to the growth rate in 2000 (0.012), there could have been about 750 million people at the time of the Flood. However, given the extremely long lifespans prior to the Flood, the growth rate could have been much higher. Increasing the rate by just 0.001 would have put the population at close to four billion at the Flood."[6]

Only eight people survived the flood. Let that sink in. I'm not saying that to cause people to live in fear. That was a special time of judgment unlike any seen since. But Jesus did say, "For the coming of the Son of Man will be just like the days of Noah" (Matthew 24:37 NASB). God is going to judge mankind again—the saved and the unsaved. I hope what follows will be a wakeup call for many who read this book.

CHAPTER 2

THE NAKED CHURCH

"Clothes make the man. Naked people have little or no influence on society."

—MARK TWAIN

Many Bible scholars believe that the letters of the seven churches mentioned in Revelation 2-3 were not only addressed to those present-day churches then, but are also representative of seven different periods in the historical timeline of the church. The last, Laodicea, being representative of the Church in the last days of the Church Age.

I find it interesting that Jesus did not have one positive thing to say about the Church of Laodicea. If ever there was a picture of the present-day Church, especially here in America, the Church at Laodicea certainly fits the bill. Many in the Church today are like the emperor with no clothes on. The enemy has convinced us that we are dressed royally when in fact we are naked of any holiness; our spiritual clothes, if we have any at all, are filthy rags full of holes. "There is a class of people who are pure in their own eyes, and yet are not washed from their own filth" (Proverbs 30:12).

The last thing that many in the Church today are doing is clothing Christ with glory and honor by the way they live. In Ezekiel 36:22-23 (MSG), God told Ezekiel that "Wherever they went, they gave me a bad name . . . I suffered much pain over my holy reputation, which the people of Israel blackened in every country they entered." Later, in Ezekiel 43:8 (MSG), God said, "they dragged my holy name through the mud . . ." and then He asked the question: "Is it any wonder that I destroyed them in anger?"

I am a strong believer in the imminent return of Christ which will close out the present church age. Based on all that Jesus had to say about the last days, as well as what is recorded in the rest of the Bible, both Old Testament and New Testament, we are living on the very cusp of Christ's return for His Bride, the Church. In the Bible, it describes the Bride that Jesus is coming back for: ". . . Christ also loved the church and gave Himself up for her, so that He might sanctify her, having cleansed her by the washing of water with the word, that He might present to Himself the church in all her glory, having no spot or wrinkle or any such thing; but that she would be holy and blameless" (Ephesians 5:25-27 NASB).

HOLINESS

As Christians we are to be holy "because it is written: 'YOU SHALL BE HOLY, FOR I AM HOLY'" (1 Peter 1:16 NASB). When was the last time you heard a message on holiness preached in your church, or in any church?

The writer to the Hebrews says, "... pursue that consecration and holiness without which no one will [ever] see the Lord" (Hebrews 12:14b).

There is a passage of scripture that has stirred a passion within me to write about holiness. It is found in Matthew 7:21-23:

> *"Not everyone who says to Me, Lord, Lord, will enter the kingdom of heaven, but he who does the will of My Father Who is in heaven.*
>
> *"Many will say to Me on that day, Lord, Lord, have we not prophesied in Your name and driven out demons in Your name and done many mighty works in Your name?*
>
> *"And then I will say to them openly (publicly), I never knew you; depart from Me, you who act wickedly [disregarding My commands].'"*

This, to me, is one of the most shocking scenes played out before us in the Bible. Can you imagine the horror that will fill the hearts of millions of people who stand before Christ and hear those awful words? Lest you think I made a mistake by saying millions, I didn't. The number will be legion who think everything is right between them and God but are not, for they have been deceived. There will be pastors, deacons, choir members, Sunday school teachers, worship leaders, and people whose names are in church roles that will hear these awful words from the mouth of the One whom they declared they loved.

"God's temple is sacred—and you, remember, *are* the temple" (1 Corinthians 3:17 MSG).

To anyone reading this I would like for you to answer this question: Do you see yourself living as holy as God would have you live? If we are honest with ourselves, I don't think any of us could answer affirmatively. I don't say that to guilt trip you.

It's been said that the largest room in the world is the room for improvement. Here is our dilemma. The closer we get to Christ and the more we are in His Word, the more we are inclined to cry out like Isaiah, "Woe is me!" The closer we get to Christ, the unholier we feel. If you can go through everyday life without feeling the conviction of sin and without any concern for where you will spend eternity, then Satan has you right where he wants you.

A good illustration of what I'm trying to convey is the example of being in a darkened room on a bright, sunshiny day. If you open the blinds, suddenly you will be aware of dust particles floating in the air. That's what the Word of God does when we let its light shine into the deepest, darkest recesses of our hearts. Things we were unaware of that are not pleasing to God, are now exposed and causing us to cry out for His cleansing.

"God's holiness pervades His entire being and shapes all His attributes. His love is a holy love, His mercy is holy mercy, and even His anger and wrath are holy anger and holy wrath."[7]

The problem that many Christians have is their concept or understanding of the importance of holiness and what it means. To many it's not that big of a deal—but with God, it's a big, big deal. "Therefore be imitators of God [copy Him *and* follow His example]" (Ephesians 5:1).

SIGNIFICANCE OF FIRST IMPRESSIONS

There used to be an old maxim that we don't hear much anymore in our casual society—the saying "dress for success." "Now, new research out of Princeton is adding yet another item to the long list of weird biases you need to look out for when you're hiring or job hunting. Even incredibly subtle differences in your clothing can affect how people judge your competence, the series of studies found, and these impressions form in under a second.

"A suit, you might think, is just a suit. As long as someone shows up to a job interview neatly turned out in role appropriate attire, then the finer details of the suit (or hoodie) wouldn't matter. But when the Princeton team placed identical faces with slightly different outfits together, they found people rated their perceived competence much differently.

"Specifically, when the clothes in question appeared subtly more expensive, whether the article of clothing in question was a suit or a T-shirt, people's perception of the wearer's confidence shot up."[8]

If we are going to clothe God with glory and honor as His representatives, then we must take on His attributes. We must clothe ourselves in holiness first.

TRUE HOLINESS

Here is the litmus test for whether you are pursuing true holiness or false holiness. If your holiness is focused on you, then it is a false holiness. When we focus on ourselves, we are concerned with what others think about us, and on how they view us.

The true definition of holiness is that we are focused on God. To a great extent, our love for God determines how holy we are. We obey Him and keep His commandments because we love Him. That is why He must be our main focus in life.

In all actuality, I rarely give any thought to holiness on my part. My focus is not on trying to be holy, it's on trying to love Him the best I possibly can. What drives me is loving and pleasing Him. So, that's why the question I ask myself isn't, "Should I do this or not," it's instead, "but would Jesus do this, say this, watch this, or participate in this?"

In life, if someone is good or great at something, what does it generally indicate? It's that they love whatever that something is. I can guarantee you that if you see a great golfer, it's because he genuinely loves the game, because you will be looking at someone that has spent thousands of hours in practice. In that same way, if you see a great builder, it's because he has applied his entire life's devotion to building beautiful edifices.

However, just because we love something, doesn't mean we will be great at it. I love golf but I'm definitely not great at it. Hopefully, the reason I'm not great at it is not because I can't become good, but because I don't have the time nor the money to practice and receive professional help to do so.

With this concept in mind, I have great news for those who want to live a holy life. It's found in 2 Peter 1:3 (NASB): "for His divine power has granted to us everything pertaining to life and godliness, through the true knowledge of Him who called us by His own glory and excellence. Through these He has granted to us His precious and magnificent promises, so that by them you may become partakers of the divine nature."

Just as He made the Sabbath Day holy, He also makes us holy. But it requires cooperation on our part. The fourth commandment in the Ten Commandments (Exodus 35:8-11) states that we are not to do any work on that day. Just as God rested on the seventh day, making it different (holy), because the work of creation was complete; that's why we now cease trying to do good works in order to make ourselves different (holy) from everyone else.

HOLINESS IN ACTION

It's my firm conviction that the American Church is permeated with Christians who bear little resemblance to Jesus Christ. Is it any wonder that people don't find the Christian message attractive? For the most part, they see a minimal difference between us (the Church) and the world.

Before we can discuss what holiness looks like we must define what holiness is. The best way to define holiness is with another word, "otherness." The first time "holy" is mentioned in the Bible is in Genesis 2:3 (MSG), "God blessed the seventh day. He made it a Holy Day because on that day he rested from his work, all the creating God had done." The seventh day was set apart from the previous six days because, it was different; it's when He stopped. Later, in Leviticus 20:26 we read, "And you shall be holy to Me; for I the Lord am holy, and have separated you from the peoples, that you should be Mine."

For many, when we say someone is holy, they picture a person walking around with a halo over their head. For others who want to be holy, they are looking for a "feeling of purity within their spirit or a clean conscience." A synonym for holy is the word dedicated. Thus, we could, without harming the meaning of the above verse, write: "So you are to be 'dedicated' to me. . . ." The adjective of dedicated is: "(of a person) devoted to a task or purpose; having single-minded loyalty or integrity." So, for us to be holy, it is not about how we appear (halo) or in how we feel, but it is in what we do. We should be unwaveringly loyal, faithfully true, dyed-in-the-wool, through and through, wholeheartedly single-minded, enthusiastically eager, keenly in earnest, zealously driven, ardently passionate, fanatically hard-working, and act as blood-bought children of King Jesus! This is because it's exactly what He wants from us.

Now, here's the really great news! He says the same thing to us in the above verse as paraphrased, "For I the Lord am holy, (dedicated) to you, and have set you apart from all other peoples to be mine." In other words, "He is unwaveringly loyal . . . to us as His blood bought children." He isn't saying, "Do as I say, not as I do." He is saying that everything I want from you I am going to give back to you in spades.

Holiness is not just an appearance or a feeling, it is an action. Another way of saying it is, "How do you spell holiness? It is spelled A.C.T.I.O.N." When we give our hearts (action) to the Lord we become followers (action) of Christ.

We've all seen it on TV or in movies, especially when they show bloopers. Here, a board they snapped before the scene is shown. It is called a clapperboard, or a slate board, and, among other things, it's used to make syncing audio and film easier; it also helps to identify takes and scenes. Then the director calls out, "Action."

When we give our hearts to Jesus, and make Him the Lord of our lives, there should be an immediate role reversal. From that point on our lives should sync up with our confession. The god(s) we once served—Satan, self, money, lust, anger, pride, the love of this world, etc.—are replaced by our love for the one and only true God. At that seminal moment, there comes a clarion call from the ramparts of heaven: "ACTION!"

Just as I spelled "holiness" equals "ACTION" I now spell "ACTION" equals "OBEDIENCE" since holiness equals acts of obedience. Jesus said, "If you [really] love Me, you will keep *and* obey My commandments (John 14:15)." If you obey someone, you either start doing something or stop doing something when they tell you to. When we accept Jesus as our Lord and Savior, we are called to stop living the way we used too, and to start living the way He calls us to live.

WHAT WOULD JESUS DO?

Ranking as one of the greatest Christian classics of all time, with over fifty million copies sold, is the book *In His Steps: What Would Jesus Do?* by Charles M. Sheldon. He began writing this book for his Sunday night services, and started by releasing one chapter a week. He challenged his congregation to not do anything for a whole year without first asking themselves the question, "What would Jesus do?"

If all of us as Christians ask ourselves the same question every day for the rest of our lives, Christianity would be a whole lot more appealing to those who are lost. Each day, when facing a decision, whether great or small, ask yourself: *Would Jesus say that? Would Jesus watch that? Would Jesus listen to that? Would Jesus take part in that? Would Jesus entertain those thoughts? Would Jesus give in to that desire? Would Jesus pray for that person that did Him wrong? Would Jesus forgive that person? Would Jesus feed, clothe, or give money, to help those people? Would Jesus visit that person in the hospital, nursing home, or in prison, to encourage them and pray for them?*

Is all of this asking or demanding too much from us? Jesus didn't think so. "Hence, when He [Christ] entered into the world, He said, sacrifices and offerings You have not desired, but instead You have made ready a body for Me [to offer]; in burnt offerings and sin offerings You have taken no delight. Then I said, Behold, here I am, coming to do Your will, O God—[to fulfill] what is written of Me in the volume of the Book" (Hebrews 10:5-7). He was willing to give us His all.

God the Father asked Jesus to sacrifice His life for our sin. At the last supper, just before departing to Gethsemane, He told His disciples, "I'll not be talking with you much more like this because the chief of this godless world is about to attack. But don't worry—he has nothing on me, no claim on me. But so, the world might know how thoroughly I love the Father, I am carrying out my Father's instructions right down to the last detail" (John 14:29-31 MSG). He asks of us that same type of sacrifice. That's how the world will know that we love Jesus—when we carry out His commandments down to the last detail.

CHAPTER 3

BLESSINGS OF OBEDIENCE

And all these blessings shall come upon you and overtake you if you heed the voice of the Lord your God.

—Deuteronomy 28:2

Someone once said that people today want to know God's will, but not in order to do it, instead in order to consider it. What is your first reaction to the word commandment? Is it positive or negative?

Generally, we tend to view commandments as something negative because we have to do something whether we like it or not. In the military, soldiers have to follow orders, and if they don't, they can be court-martialed and thrown in the brig. That mentality can carry over to the commandments in God's Word. Our attitude can be "we have to keep His commandments." But it's a negative mindset in how we see them rather than us viewing them as something positive. So, what we must realize is that God's commandments are positive, and that they are accompanied by promises and blessings. God doesn't want us to obey Him just because He's God. He wants us to obey Him so that He might bless us and give us His exceedingly great promises. We understand the greatness of God's commandments when we realize that they are not binding, but freeing.

Here are some examples of that truth. In John 15:10-11, Jesus promises us that if we obey His commands we will abide in His love, His joy will remain in us, and our joy will be full. In other words, we will experience an intimacy that is like no other with the One who created us, and we will be filled with what the apostle Peter describes as "... joy inexpressible and full of glory" (1 Peter 1:8 NASB).

Nehemiah gives us another benefit by telling us, " ... the joy of the Lord is your strength and stronghold" (Nehemiah 8:10). So we see in these scriptures that obedience equals intimacy, joy, and strength.

The reason we are here today is because Noah obeyed the Lord and built an ark. So, if we obey Him, we too can be the reason all of our family is saved. Obedience equals escape from God's wrath.

Abraham is another great example of what can happen when we obey the Lord. "And in your seed all the nations of the earth shall be blessed, because you have obeyed My voice" (Genesis 22:18 NASB). Obedience equals exponential blessings.

Moses obeyed the Lord and as a result, the Israelites were delivered from bondage. If we obey the Lord's command to be His witnesses, many will be set free from slavery to sin. Obedience equals freedom.

Because Paul obeyed God, God used him to write almost a quarter of the New Testament. Obedience equals fulfillment of purpose.

BLESSINGS OF OBEDIENCE

Most of the commandments that Jesus gave in the Sermon on the Mount were immediately followed by promises or rewards. Beginning in verse 25, and also in verses 32-33, He tells us, "If you decide for God, living a life of God-worship, it follows that you don't fuss about what's on the table at mealtimes or whether the clothes in your closet are in fashion.... What I'm trying to do here is to get you to relax, to not be so preoccupied with *getting*, so you can respond to God's *giving*. People who don't know God and the way he works fuss over these things, but you know both God and how he works. Steep your life in God reality, God-initiative, God-provisions" (Matthew 6:25, 31-32 MSG). Obedience equals all of our needs being met.

First John 4:17-18 (MSG) says, "God is love. When we take up permanent residence in a life of love, we live in God and God lives in us. This way, love has the run of the house, becomes at home and mature in us, so that we're free of worry on Judgment Day—our standing in the world is identical with Christ's. There is no room in love for fear. Well-formed love banishes fear. Since fear is crippling, a fearful life—fear of death, fear of judgment—is one not yet fully formed in love."

If we are like Jesus in this world then we have no fear of the future, no matter what it brings, and ultimately, we will live with Him in heaven in eternity. Obedience equals absence of fear.

CHAPTER 4

IS CLOTHING OPTIONAL?

"There is no justification without sanctification, no forgiveness without renewal of life, no real faith from which the fruits of new obedience do not grow."

—MARTIN LUTHER

Those around my age, seventy-two, will remember the signs in the windows of businesses that said, "No shoes, no shirt, no service." I can see in my mind's eye the signs posted on the twelve gates of the New Jerusalem bearing this message, "Without holiness no one will enter these gates!"

As I mentioned earlier, the definition of holiness is "otherness." As Christians we should be different from nonbelievers. In order to have a clearer understanding of what follows, it is necessary to add a little meat to the bones of holiness. By that I mean that there is what some refer to as "positional sanctification" and "progressive sanctification."

POSITIONAL SANCTIFICATION

Positional sanctification is what we become when we put our faith in Jesus Christ and make Him the Lord of our lives. We are sanctified and made holy in Him. We see this in Titus 3:5-7 (NASB): "He saved us, not on the basis of deeds which we did in righteousness, but in accordance with His mercy, by the washing of regeneration and renewing by the Holy Spirit, whom He richly poured out upon us through Jesus Christ our Savior, so that being justified by His grace we would be made heirs according to the hope of eternal life." The key word here is justified. I've heard it said this way: "justified—just as if we had never sinned." It's in this moment in time, where we make that confession of faith, that we are made holy, as if we had never sinned.

PROGRESSIVE SANCTIFICATION

Paul follows up "positional sanctification" with what follows in verse 8 (NASB): "This statement is trustworthy; and concerning these things I want you to speak confidently, so that those who have believed God will be careful to engage in good deeds." This is progressive sanctification. This is observable holiness. There should be an obvious change in us. We were going one way, but now we are going the opposite way. This is where born-again believers are different from the world.

IS CLOTHING OPTIONAL?

Now, to be clear, this takes effort on our part. Paul says it this way: "For we are His workmanship, created in Christ Jesus for good works, which God prepared beforehand so that we would walk in them" (Ephesians 2:10 NASB). The good news is God through His Spirit supplies the grace we need to live out lives of holiness. "Christ's life showed me how and enabled me to do it. I identified myself completely with him. Indeed, I have been crucified with Christ. My ego is no longer central. It is no longer important that I appear righteous before you or have your good opinion, and I am no longer driven to impress God. Christ lives in me. The life you see me living is not 'mine,' but it is lived by faith in the Son of God, who loved me and gave himself for me" (Galatians 2:20 MSG).

I love the way Jessica Van Roekel expressed this truth. "We do not drift into spiritual maturity. We determine to cooperate with the power of God that is within us."[9] Think about this quote in the context of Titus 3:5, " . . . not on the basis of deeds which we did in righteousness." The Holy Spirit showed me that we do not do good works in order to be righteous, we do good works as a result of being made righteous in Christ.

What follows next is a look at the nuts-and-bolts of positional sanctification and progressive sanctification. What I'm about to write may be misunderstood as a desire to return to legalism in the church, where holiness is defined by outward appearance and actions rather than what comes from the heart. That's the last place I want to return to.

We need to ask ourselves two questions. Who or what is our focus? The second is what are our motives?

Were you alive when almost everyone who attended church in America dressed up in their "Sunday best?" Suits and dresses were the norm. Now, for most men, it's the casual look, jeans, t-shirts, and for some men (especially younger men), it's shorts and flip-flops. Women attending church are not as inclined to be as casual as men. Often, they are comfortably dressed in jeans and sandals. Although, there are some women who tend to be a little too casual with wearing low cut tops and short skirts or shorts that are too short. I know of a pastor who instructed the church maintenance supervisor to lower the temperature during the summer in an attempt to discourage women from dressing too scantily.

When did America start to get too casual and why?

On August 5, 2015, *Time Magazine* released an article by Deirdre Clemente who addressed these questions. As a professor she teaches seminars on "material culture" with a focus on the why and when "our sartorial standards went from collared to comfortable." It first began in the 1920s. "As Americans, our casual style uniformly stresses comfort and practicality—two words that have gotten little attention in the history of fashion but have transformed how we live."

She goes on to write, "Americans dress casual. Why? Because clothes are freedom—freedom to choose how we present ourselves to the world; freedom to blur the lines between man and woman, old and young, rich and poor. The rise of casual style directly undermined millennia-old rules that dictated noticeable luxury for the rich and functioning work clothes for the poor. Until a little more than a century ago, there were very few ways to disguise your social class. You wore it—literally—on your sleeve. Today, CEOs wear sandals to work and white suburban kids tweak their L.A. Raiders hat a little too far to the side. Compliments of global capitalism, the clothing market is flooded with options to mix-and-match to create a personal style."[10]

IS IT LEGALISM OR REVERENCE?

I feel compelled to consider first what the Old Testament says about God's servants. The Old Testament has much to say about how the Israelites were to approach God. Not only did the Law have much to say about how the priests and Levites were to worship and serve God but it also spelled out the requirements and restrictions placed upon the congregation of Israel as a whole.

The Bible says that "Jesus Christ is the same yesterday and today, and forever (Hebrews 13:8 NASB)." Many, if not most Bible scholars, believe it was pre-incarnate Jesus Christ that gave the law to Moses on Mount Sinai. In Exodus 28:2, pre-incarnate Jesus instructs Moses to make Aaron, the high priest, some beautiful clothes. Beginning with verse 4 and going all the way through verse 39, God gave Moses extremely specific instructions on how Aaron was to be dressed. Beginning with verse 40-43, God then instructs Moses on how Aaron's sons were to be dressed. These same rules applied to their descendants as well.

If God would dedicate an entire chapter in His Word to clothes, could that be an indicator of the importance of how we dress ourselves outwardly? Today we attend church in extremely casual wear in the summer. If you happen to live in an area where you have a great sports team the congregation doesn't leave any doubt on game day as to where their loyalty lies.

In 2022, the global sports apparel market was around 200 billion dollars. If you think I'm just a sour puss when it comes to sports, that's not so. I love those Chiefs! I do distinctly remember though what Jesus said in Matthew 6:21: "for where your treasure is, there your heart will be also." When we are in church could our clothes be indicative of where our focus is?

I mentioned earlier that we are ambassadors for Christ and that God makes His appeal through us. If United States ambassadors to foreign countries are expected to dress in a dignified way while in office, shouldn't we, who are ambassadors of the King of Kings, dress in a manner that reflects well upon the One we serve too? In creation God made all things beautiful. However, sin corrupted that beauty. Shouldn't we, as His representatives, play our small part in restoring that beauty to His creation?

You may be inclined to say, "That's the Old Testament and that had to do with the Law. We are no longer under the Law, we're under grace." That's true, but if we are to ignore the Old Testament, as some do to their great detriment, then the New Testament makes no sense.

In the New Testament, the types, precepts, and truths of the Old Testament are explained and applied to those of us who are living in the dispensation of grace, and under the New Covenant. Peter writes in 1 Peter 1:15-16 (MSG), "As obedient children, let yourselves be pulled into a way of life shaped by God's life, a life energetic and blazing with holiness. God said, 'I am holy; you be holy.'" In verse 16, Peter is quoting from Leviticus 11:44.

God's expectations of His people living holy lives has not changed now that we are born again believers. The difference now is explained by the apostle Paul in Ephesians: "For it is by free grace (God's unmerited favor) that you are saved (delivered from judgment *and* made partakers of Christ's salvation) through [your] faith. And this [salvation] is not of yourselves [of your own doing, it came not through your own striving], but it is the gift of God; Not because of works [not the fulfillment of the Law's demands], lest any man should boast. [It is not the result of what anyone can possibly do, so no one can pride himself in it or take glory to himself]" (Ephesians 2:8-9). That's an Old Testament precept (truth) applied under the New Covenant.

The precept in the Old Testament is still the same, it's just carried out in a new way. It's accomplished through grace, mercy, and the power of the indwelling Spirit of Christ within us, that enables us to live lives of holiness.

IT'S THE LITTLE THINGS

Continuing the discussion on clothing, casual attire began to show up in the church in the 1960s. Some would say it was a result of the Jesus movement which brought an influx of hippies into the traditional church setting. I remember when the church I attended began to go casual. The reason given was that we didn't want anyone, no matter what their status in life, to feel uncomfortable when attending our church. One of the concerns was that those who couldn't afford nice clothes would not come for fear of standing out like a sore thumb.

For those my age, or closer to it, it is obvious that church culture has changed dramatically over the years. The serious questions I raise now are these: Is it for the better, or is there something more insidious going on? Have we lost a reverence for the house of God? Is it indicative that we don't fear God or the things of God like our parents and grandparents did? Did they mistakenly put too much emphasis on the outward appearance? Could our casual dress translate into a more casual relationship with the God of all creation?

With coffee and sometimes food in hand, we enter the auditorium and settle comfortably into our seats with our phones turned on in case someone calls or texts, ready to be entertained. This is all too often fostered by leaders in the churches, especially mega-churches, where the focus is inspired by the secular entertainment industry; their motto focuses only on the best graphics, music, lights, and the best speakers. Don't get me wrong. Just as it's not about clothes, my focus is not on graphics, music, lights, and the best speakers. My wife and I attended a mega church before we moved to our present home. They employed all of these means as tools to carry out their main goal—reaching the lost. Our pastor's main emphasis was, and still is, the Word of God, and salvation of the lost.

Many reading this may say I'm overreacting, or going to the extreme with what I'm saying, and with what I'm about to say next. I mentioned above that there may be something more insidious at play here. Could it be that, over the years, the enemy of our souls, Satan, has led the church down the slippery slope towards the blurring of the lines of all that is true and holy? One of the tools in his toolbox that he uses very effectively is incrementalism. "A little sleep, a little slumber, A little folding of the hands to rest ..." (Proverbs 24:33 NASB). He gets us to let down our guard, using sayings like, "It's not that important! That's just a little thing. It's so insignificant!" Satan is a long-range planner. He's had centuries to implement his schemes.

Legalism, in the past, implied that the way we dressed showed how holy we were. However, I can't stress this enough. Dressing nicely when we go to church isn't a matter of holiness, but an expression of our love, reverence, and our desire to honor the Lord as His representatives.

I struggled with the change at the time but I was fully on-board with the focus of changed lives through the Gospel of Jesus Christ, rather than with the change of attire. Does all of this mean that there should be little, if any, concern about what we wear as Christians when we attend church?

I want to leave you with this question to mull over. What would you do if you were Satan and you wanted to diminish the reverence and awe given to God by His people? Wouldn't it be like Satan to give a seemingly good spiritual reason to start them down that path by stripping them of reasons to wear presentable and nice clothes? He'd probably say things like, "You don't want to keep people who can't afford to dress nicely from coming to church do you?"

The Song of Solomon speaks of the little foxes that spoil the vines. "[My heart was touched, and I fervently sang to him my desire] Take for us the foxes, the little foxes that spoil the vineyards [of our love], for our vineyards are in blossom" (Song of Solomon 2:15). Satan couches his schemes in spiritual language. It's the little things that can lead to bigger issues. Isn't it possible that if Satan can get us to relax our standards in one area of our life, then he can move on to other areas until we have little, if any, standards at all?

You may be thinking that I'm making a big deal out of nothing. That all I'm doing is trying to get us back into legalism.

IMPORTANCE OF ATTIRE

I read two interesting articles recently on the same subject, the importance of how we dress. The first is by Scott Raines and is titled *Perspective: The Dressing Down of America*. In it, he tells the story of U.S. Senator John Fetterman returning to the Senate after being released from treatment for clinical depression.

"Fetterman stepped out of his car and greeted onlookers in workout shorts, gray sneakers, and a baggy Carhartt sweatshirt. His look, or lack thereof, caused an uproar on social media. And rightfully so." Mr. Raines went on to quote Saagar Enjeti, a co-host of the podcast *Breaking Points*. "People who buck proper dress code at the highest levels of public service are narcissists who think their personal comfort/'brand' supersedes decorum. They're not trying to relate; they think they're above everyone else."

Mr. Raines goes on to say, "We act as if dress isn't important. But what we wear isn't simply a matter of decorum; rather, it reflects one's heart and metaphysical well-being. How one dresses the body mirrors the soundness of the soul and the mind, and signals respect for both the beauty of the world and those who live in it."

In this article he also quotes Esme Partridge who is a writer and consultant working between religion, philosophy, and politics. Listen to what she says about all of this: "The decline in contemporary style is commonly accepted as 'going goblin mode,' saying that 'teenagers today are doing away with all ideals. . . . They like their celebrities upholding hardly any standards at all."

My final quote from the article raises what I believe to be a serious question for the church world. "I see the cultural inversion in my university students who come to class looking like models in a Hanes underwear commercial. Rarely do I see a student well-dressed and put together, having made the morning sacrifice to dress as if he or she had some sense of personal self-worth. Most students are content to show up and feel "comfy"—the anthem of contemporary fashion."[11]

The second interesting article I read was an opinion piece written by Peggy Noonan on September 21, 2023, in the *Wall Street Journal* titled *The Senator's Shorts and America's Decline*. The line that stuck out most to me was this: "We want to be respected, but no longer think we need to be respectable." She goes on to say: "We are in a crisis of political comportment. We are witnessing the rise of the classless. Our politicians are becoming degenerate. This has been happening for a while but gets worse as the country coarsens. We are defining deviancy ever downward." She wrote the article in response to what Senate Majority Leader Chuck Schumer did, apparently in response to the above-mentioned Senator John Fetterman's choice of attire. In her words, "He quietly swept away a century-old tradition that senators dress as adults on the floor of the senate. Business attire is no longer formally required."

She then gives a list of reasons, which I will try to shorten to one line per reason, of why John Fetterman, as well as all the other senators, should adhere to certain standards.

It shows respect for colleagues.

It shows respect for the institution.

You are a public servant; servants by definition make sacrifices.

It reflects an inner discipline. The effort means you bothered, took the time, and went to the trouble.

It reflects an inner modesty.

It bows to the ideas of standards itself.

It shows that you understand that America now has a problem with showing respect.

It shows that you admit to yourself that part of your job is to model how to behave for those who are younger.

It shows you don't think you're better than others. News reporters, citizens who testify before congress, and Senate staffers, must all still abide by the old dress code.

It shows that, as a high elected official of the United States, you owe the country, and the world, the outward signs of maturity, judgment, and earnestness. That isn't asking too much. It is a baseline minimum.

She finishes her article with this statement, "How people bear themselves has implications greater than we know. It's not about 'sartorial choice.' It's about who we need you to be—and who you asked to be when you first ran."[12]

Now, these are secular writers saying this, not those necessarily concerned with spiritual matters. If they view the way we dress as a society as indicative of lowering our standards, then how is it that the Church of Jesus Christ is not bothered by the way that we, the people of God, present ourselves when we come into the presence of an Almighty God?

To any and all who are reading this, please don't infer that I'm judging you by what you wear to church or anywhere else. My purpose is not to condemn or make you feel guilty. Satan is the author of condemnation. Jesus himself said in John 3:17 (NASB), "For God did not send His Son into the world to judge the world, but so that the world might be saved through Him." The Holy Spirit doesn't condemn either, He only convicts. "And He, when He comes, will convict the world regarding sin, and righteousness, and judgment" (John 16:8 NASB). One of the purposes of the Holy Spirit is to bring the conviction of sin in our lives that we try to cover up, ignore, or make excuses for. None of this is my business, it's only between you and God.

MINDSET

On May 17, 2014, Admiral William H. McRaven gave a commencement speech to the graduating class of the University of Texas in Austin. You may have heard or seen it. He mentioned the University's slogan which states "What starts here changes the world." He told them if they wanted to change the world, the first thing they needed to do in the morning when they got up was to make their bed. "If you make your bed every morning you will have accomplished the first task of the day. It will give you a small sense of pride, and it will encourage you to do another task and another and another. By the end of the day, that one task completed will have turned into many tasks completed. Making your bed will also reinforce the fact that little things in life matter. If you can't do the little things right, you will never do the big things right."[13]

When you think of God, what do you think of in regard to His creation? In Genesis 1:10, on speaking about His creation, it says, "And God saw that it was good." In verse 25, "And God saw that it was good." In verse 31 it says, "God saw all that he had made, and it was very good" (Genesis 1:10,25,31 NASB).

Whatever God does, it is the best and for our best. It is He who created the unlimited vastness of space and the glorious beauty of the heavens. And yet, Jesus said in speaking about flowers, "yet I say to you that not even Solomon in all his glory clothed himself like one of these. But if God so clothes the grass of the field, which is alive today and tomorrow is thrown into the furnace, will He not much more clothe you? You of little faith . . ." (Matthew 6:29-30 NASB). Could you imagine the God of all creation, the God of the Bible, ever making something less than perfect? I can't.

If we are his children and desire to be like him, should we give him anything less than our best? "Therefore, whether you eat or drink, or whatever you do, do all things for the glory of God (1 Corinthians 10:31).

FIRST CAUSE

If you're not very knowledgeable on the Bible, you may be wondering why the world is in such a mess if God is a God of perfection and beauty? I love science and I would like to use a law of nature, the second law of thermodynamics, as an illustration to answer this question.

Saibal Mitra, a professor of physics at Missouri State University, says this about the second law of thermodynamics, "At a very microscopic level, it simply says that if you have a system that is isolated, any natural process in that system progresses in the direction of increasing disorder, or entropy, of the system."[14]

Whenever you think of Satan, what do you think of in regard to him? Satan is the author of sin. Sin is destructive. Sin is the cause of disorder and chaos. Sin causes deterioration. Sin brings death. It has been said that the day we were born was the day we began to die. Our whole life is a process of dying. That's really edifying, isn't it?

God's focus was not changed when He instituted the New Covenant. The difference is that the emphasis is now more on how we clothe the inner man with spiritual clothing, rather than how we wear our outward apparel. We are to "put on the Lord Jesus Christ" (Romans 13:14 NASB; see also Galatians 3:27). "And all of you, clothe yourselves with humility toward one another" (1 Peter 5:5b NASB). In Revelation 19:8 we are clothed "in fine linen, bright and clean; for the fine linen is the righteous acts of the saints." Jesus himself clothes us in His righteousness.

I mentioned Isaiah 61:10 (NASB) which ends with, "As a bridegroom decks himself with a garland, and as a bride adorns herself with her jewels." The garland is a symbol of victory and honor. Here, it shows that Jesus is victorious over sin. Because of His victory, He imputes to us His garland of righteousness, which is perfect and beautiful. So we have a part in celebrating His victory.

HOW TO HONOR HIM

How do we honor Him greatly you ask? We, as His Bride, adorn ourselves with jewels. The really wonderful news is He provides us with those jewels. Some of those jewels are referred to as the Fruit of the Spirit in Galatians 5:22-23 (NASB), which says "But the fruit of the Spirit is love, joy, peace, forbearance, kindness, goodness, faithfulness, gentleness and self-control." The Apostle James mentions more jewels in James 3:17 (MSG) "Real wisdom, God's wisdom, begins with a holy life and is characterized by getting along with others. It is gentle and reasonable, overflowing with mercy and blessings, not hot one day and cold the next, not two-faced."

Now, here is one more example of how we clothe Christ with honor. Jesus himself speaks these words when we stand before him on judgment day. "Then the King will say to those on His right, 'Come, you who are blessed of My Father, inherit the kingdom prepared for you from the foundation of the world. For I was hungry, and you gave Me something to eat; I was thirsty, and you gave Me something to drink; I was a stranger, and you invited Me in; naked, and you clothed Me; I was sick, and you visited Me; I was in prison, and you came to Me" (Matthew 25:34-36 NASB).

I have suggested that we have a part in clothing Christ in honor and beauty. What follows next is my conviction that the Church has, to all intents and purposes, become its own worst enemy. We have fallen prey to the lies of the enemy and have sullied the glorious garments of our great God and King, and our Lord and Savior Jesus Christ, by the way we live.

CHAPTER 5

WE SERVE A GOD WHO IS TO BE FEARED

"He that has slight thoughts about sin never has great thoughts about God."

—JOHN OWEN

In the last chapter we looked at who and what was our focus. Now we need to look at who and what is our motive.

I believe our enemy, Satan, has deceived the Church. He has used our desire to relate to the world to diminish our reverence for the things of God. This discussion of how we clothe ourselves has nothing to do with legalism. It has everything to do with our perspective and mindset. The reason we have lost a reverence for the things of God is because we have lost the fear of God.

The NASB translation has Romans 3:18 in all caps. It says, "THERE IS NO FEAR OF GOD BEFORE THEIR EYES." It gives us the impression that the Holy Spirit through Paul is shouting, "Wake up people! Pay attention! Don't miss this!" In these verses Paul is describing the condition of all unregenerate mankind. His conclusion for the reason they live the way they do is because they have no fear of God. I personally think there should have been an exclamation point at the end of verse 18, maybe several.

Probably the most familiar verse in the Bible that's about fear is found in Proverbs 9:10 (NASB): "The fear of the LORD is the beginning of wisdom, and the knowledge of the Holy One is understanding."

In the past, I have labored under the mistaken notion that when the Bible says that we are to "fear God" it simply means that we are to regard or treat Him with great respect. Many times I've heard preachers, teachers, and others who emphatically say that when the Bible says to fear God, it doesn't mean that we should be afraid of God; He doesn't want us to be afraid of Him, he just wants us to be in awe of Him, and to greatly respect Him. I disagree.

Most commentaries also say the same thing. Here are just three examples:

> "The word "fear" that is used here denotes "reverence, awe, veneration." (*Barnes Notes on the Whole Bible*)."[15]
>
> "A reverential awe of Him with whom we have to do . . ." (*Jamieson-Fausset-Brown Bible Commentary*)."[16]

"A reverential affection for God . . ." (*Gill's Exposition of the Entire Bible*).[17]

By giving these illustrations, it is not an attempt to denigrate these great men of God. I hold them in high esteem. If you were to think that I am placing my understanding of Scripture on their level, that would be foolishness on my part. I'm just taking the teaching of my former pastor, which I think is correct, and expanding on it.

If that is the case, then what are we to do with this verse? "And do not be afraid of those who kill the body but are unable to kill the soul; but rather fear Him who is able to destroy both soul and body in hell" (Matthew 10:28 NASB). The Greek word used here is *"mowra"* – "by implication, a fearful thing or deed, dread, (that ought to be) fear(-ed), terribleness, terror."[18] Jesus is saying we have a reason to be afraid, to dread, or to be in terror of Him if we are not living in obedience to His Word.

The only one who can destroy both soul and body in hell is God. Jesus says be afraid of Him. As shown above it's more than just being afraid, we should be in terror of Him for He is a God Who can cast us into hell for eternity.

How do you think Aaron, and all of the high priests that followed him, on the Day of Atonement when they went into the Holy of Holies to offer atonement for the nation of Israel, would respond if they were asked if they just respected Him (God), or if they were trembling in fear?

Twice in Leviticus 16 God warned the priest to follow all of the instructions given prior to entering the Holy of Holies. The penalty was death if he entered into the Shekinah glory of God's presence without his sins being atoned for properly.

According to tradition a rope was tied around their ankle so their body could be removed if the High Priest was struck dead. Since only the High Priest could enter the Holy of Holies, another priest would be standing in the Holy Place holding on to the other end of the rope to pull his body out.

I can assure you that rope tied around his ankle was a reminder that he wasn't to just casually saunter into the inner sanctum. I know if I were him, I would be like Santa Claus. I would be making a list and checking it twice, to make sure I covered all the requirements.

HEAVENLY BEINGS

Another good example of a natural response from someone who is suddenly in the presence of God is seen in Revelation 1:10,17: "I was in the Spirit [rapt in His power] on the Lord's Day, and I heard behind me a great voice like the calling of a war trumpet.... When I saw Him, I fell at His feet as if dead. But He laid His right hand on me and said, 'Do not be afraid!'"

John was chosen by Jesus Himself to be an apostle of Christ. He had spent three and a half years in close fellowship with Jesus while He was here on this earth, and yet when Jesus appeared to him in His glorified state, John went down like he had been hit with a two-by-four. Even though we may be a committed disciple of Christ, our natural response would still be terror if we were to come into the manifested presence of Christ.

And why wouldn't we respond like that when God Himself, while speaking to the prophet Ezekiel says, "The fish of the sea, the birds of the sky, the animals of the field, all the crawling things that crawl on the earth, and all mankind who are on the face of the earth will shake at My presence; and the mountains will be thrown down, the steep pathways will collapse, and every wall will fall to the ground" (Ezekiel 38:20 NASB).

WHY IS THERE NO FEAR?

When people my age see the increase in crime and vulgarness of the day in which we live, we tend to wish for the "good old days," and for good reason. We've all seen rioters spitting on police officers and destroying property with impunity. We've seen videos of the police being beaten in the streets, with gangs invading businesses in "smash and grabs," while people walk into stores and calmly steal what they want because they know they won't be prosecuted for crimes committed that are less than $1,000 in value. The reason they do this is because, across America, there are progressive prosecutors who have gone soft on crime by ending cash bail and not prosecuting shoplifters.

What happens as a result is that the police are frustrated when they see criminals they arrested earlier in the day back on the streets continuing to commit the same crimes. Not only that, but these same progressive prosecutors will charge police with criminal charges when a criminal loses their life while committing one. This happens even when the police follow standard operating procedures. Police are becoming afraid that they may end up being sentenced to years in prison while trying to protect public safety. Their future freedoms can be on the line when they are forced to make split-second judgments.

I recently read a story on npr.org about "a St. Louis homicide detective named Roger Murphey. He is refusing to testify in murder cases in which he was the lead investigator. So far, he's declined to take the stand in at least nine cases. And Murphey thinks his absence hurt prosecutors' chances of getting convictions."

The article goes on to report why he wouldn't testify in these cases: "Because the St. Louis prosecutor's office put Murphey on a list of police officers with credibility problems. Murphey landed on it, he believes unfairly, because of some Facebook posts interpreted as being racist. But even though Murphey was on that list, the prosecutor's office still asked him to testify in cases. Murphey says it's hypocritical to question his integrity yet trust him to take the stand. And he says if he does testify, defense lawyers might attack him about why he's on the list, so he's not doing it."[19]

You may be wondering why I've gone off on a rant about the rise in crime. So let me bring it home spiritually with this verse: "Because the sentence against an evil deed is not executed quickly, therefore the hearts of the sons of mankind among them are fully given to do evil" (Ecclesiastes 8:11 NASB).

When messages from the pulpits of America are espousing the incredibleness of God's grace, mercy, and forgiveness, without the juxtaposition of the Holiness of God, that He is a God of Justice, and that there isn't immediate judgment of sin, Satan can lull the uninformed parishioner into thinking that everything's okay between them and God when it's not.

"Who talked you into the pursuit of this nonsense, leaving me high and dry, forgetting you ever knew me? Because I don't yell and make a scene, do you think I don't exist? I'll go over, detail by detail, all your 'righteous' attempts at religion, and expose the absurdity of it all" (Isaiah 57:11-12 MSG).

WE SERVE A GOD WHO IS TO BE FEARED

The French saying that has to do with economics comes to my mind when thinking of the average Christian's view of sin is *"laissez faire,"* which means, "allow to do." In other words, because there are no immediate consequences, and because God is a God of mercy, grace, and forgiveness, then it's not a big deal when we sin. We're allowed to do it because of God's amazing grace.

In God's economy God's amazing grace is just that—amazing! But hold on, Peter has something to say about this. "FOR THE EYES OF THE LORD ARE TOWARD THE RIGHTEOUS, AND HIS EARS ATTEND TO THEIR PRAYER" (1 Peter 3:12a NASB).

It's an awesome truth that if we are wholly committed in our obedience to Christ, it means He is constantly watching us, and He will hear our prayers when we cry out to Him to perfect His holiness within us.

One of my favorite prayers that I like to pray is, "Lord, help me to walk in victory, not in defeat; in power, not in weakness; in love, not in fear; and faith, not in doubt."

All of us, at one time or another when we are trying our best to walk in obedience to Christ, will still stumble and fall in moments of weakness. It's in those times where we can take great comfort in knowing He is watching our every step; when we cry out to Him, He will not only hear our cry, but will answer our prayer for forgiveness and help us to become more than conquerors through Christ Jesus.

But there is a warning to the second part of the Scripture above, "BUT THE FACE OF THE LORD IS AGAINST EVILDOERS" (1 Peter 3:12b NASB). As believers, we need to be careful not to fall into the trap where we justify our sin or make excuses.

Do people really expect the Lord to overlook when they curse, to not be offended by it when they say, "Excuse my French?" In the last couple of years, I have noticed the trend in the church of defining deviancy downward. I have met more than a few believers who cuss and drink like the proverbial sailor and have no qualms with sleeping with their girlfriend/boyfriend, or fiancé.

There are many more who feel justified in their anger, bitterness, unforgiveness, and hatred. Satan has convinced them with the lie, "If only people knew what they did to me, they would understand why I can't let that go."

But if we are coddling sin in our lives by walking in habitual sin, even though we call ourselves "believers," then we will have someone of immense power against us, the Lord Himself. What Peter wrote in 1 Peter 3:12 was actually a partial quote from Psalm 34:15-16. Here's the complete version of verse 16: "The eyes of the Lord are toward the [uncompromisingly] righteous and His ears are open to their cry. The face of the Lord is against those who do evil, to cut off the remembrance of them from the earth" (NASB).

That should make any who are reading this shake in their boots in terror if they are committing habitual sin, if they are coddling and justifying sin in their lives. God is on a mission to blot their memory from the earth.

I'm sure most of you are familiar with this verse, "I can do all things through Him who strengthens me" (Philippians 4:13 NASB). This may sound like a hollow promise to some who are reading this and who desperately want to live for God, but keep struggling with the same sin issues that keep them in bondage. Even now you may be saying "I certainly haven't found that to be true."

Here's the reason; God will not dwell in an unclean vessel. We can't expect God to set us free when He's on the outside looking in. This is an inside job. You won't experience His power to set you free if you are walking in disobedience to His commandments as it says in this verse, "For it is [not your strength, but it is] God who is effectively at work in you, both to will and to work [that is, strengthening, energizing, and creating in you the longing and the ability to fulfill your purpose] for His good pleasure" (Philippians 2:13).

Let's conclude this chapter with this quote from Charles Spurgeon: "Salvation in sin is not possible, it must always be salvation from sin."

CHAPTER 6

THE GREATEST OBSTACLE TO HOLINESS

Some fights are not worth your time—
choose what you fight for wisely.

—UNKNOWN

I'm going to say something that may shock you. Satan doesn't care if you're in church every time the doors are open. He's fine with you leading worship, singing in the choir, teaching a Sunday School class, giving generously to the church, serving on the church board, and even pastoring the church. He's fine with that as long as he can keep you—and everyone else—in bondage.

In Hebrews 12:1 it speaks of "that sin which so readily (deftly and cleverly) clings to and entangles us." There are multitudes of believers that live lives of quiet desperation, while living in spiritual defeat.

There are many believers who can sincerely say that they are much better people since making their confession of faith. They are kinder, more loving, forgiving, patient, and generous than they used to be. And yet there are still strongholds in their lives that they haven't been able to overcome, no matter how hard they try. It might be lust, greed, pride, pornography, sex outside of marriage, alcoholism, anger, hatred, foul language (cussing), etc. These may be besetting sins for you. That's why this takes us back to the question of our focus. What, or who, are we focused on?

There is wisdom in knowing what to fight for, but when we are fighting for something, or someone, we are also fighting against something or someone. In the context of this discussion, we are fighting for the honor of God and fighting against self-love.

SELF ON THE THRONE

Obedience to Christ does not come without a cost. We are called to de-throne self, crucify the flesh, take up our cross daily, and follow Him. In return He promises us rewards that are out of this world. The reality is that it is extremely easy to still be servants of our selves rather than be servants of God. This is because we have become our own God.

Satan is the author of misdirection. If he can get us to focus on the little things that keep us from living that overcoming life in Christ, he will keep us from seeing the root-cause of those "besetting sins." This can result in misdirected efforts which take up much of our time and energy. If Satan can keep us busy by putting out the little fires, then we'll never get to the source of what's feeding the flames.

One of the ways of putting out a fire is to remove the fuel (starvation). The Apostle Paul, in writing to his son in the faith, Timothy, about the last days, tells us about the source for all those "besetting sins:" "For people will be lovers of themselves" (2 Timothy 3:2). What follows in verses 2-9 are a litany of sins that emanate from self-love. If ever there was a generation that is consumed with self, it's this one. *Merriam-Webster* dictionary recognized the worldwide self-absorption and even added a new word to their publication in 2014: "selfie."

Let me give you a mental picture of our problem. There are some plants that have taproots. A taproot is a large, central, and dominant root from which others sprout laterally. As long as that taproot is "self," the roots that sprout laterally are those besetting sins; the sins of the flesh that we can never get totally free from.

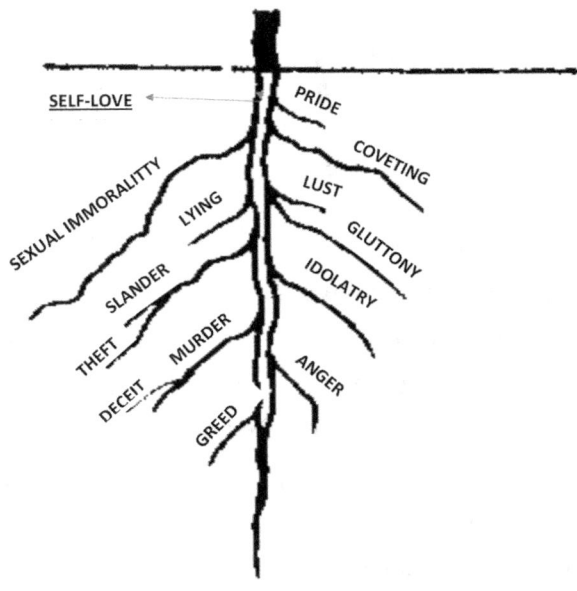

When we truly die to self, then "Among those who belong to Christ, everything connected with getting our own way and mindlessly responding to what everyone else calls necessities is killed off for good—crucified" (Galatians 5:24 MSG). If we allow ourselves to be grafted into Christ, He becomes the taproot and those roots that sprout laterally will be works of righteousness.

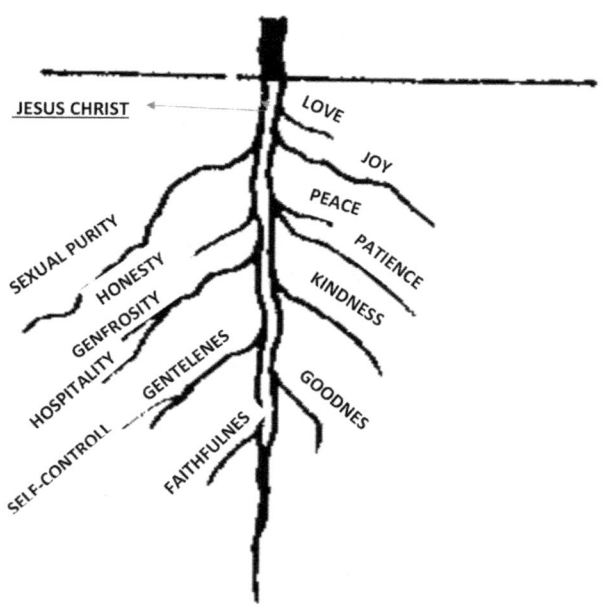

Frank Sinatra, that great spiritual giant of old [sic], gave a perfect example of the problem we have in the area of self. In a concert he held at Madison Square Garden in 1972, he introduced his next song by telling his audience that he was going to sing America's National Anthem; however, they wouldn't need to stand up. He then began singing one of his greatest hits, *My Way*. Do you remember the key phrase in that song? "I did it my way." That's not only America's national anthem, but it's also the world's. It's all about what *we* want.

THE GREATEST OBSTACLE TO HOLINESS

To continue on the same thought, "We shall discover: In our service for Christ, self-confidence and self-esteem; in the slightest suffering, self-saving and self-pity; in the least misunderstanding, self-defense and self-vindication; in our station in life, self-seeking and self-centeredness; in the smallest trials, self-inspection and self-accusation; in the daily routine, self-pleasing and self-choosing; in our relationships, self-assertiveness and self-respect; in our education, self-boasting and self-expression; in our desires, self-indulgence and self-satisfaction; in our successes, self-admiration and self-congratulations; in our failures, self-excusing, and self-justification; in our spiritual attainments, self-righteousness and self-complacency; in our public ministry, self-reflection and self-glory; in life as a whole, self-love, and selfishness. The flesh is an 'I' specialist. You are sensitive, thin skinned? Why not call it sinful pride? The next time somebody reproves you, just say, 'You don't know half the truth. If you knew me, you would say much worse.' This may help you into harmony with the Cross. It will at least be the truth."[20]

The greatest promoter of self-awareness is Satan. If he can get us to focus on ourselves instead of Christ, then he has us right where he wants us. The sad truth is that Satan uses, among other things, Christian psychologists to promote his schemes.

Paul Brownback in his book, *The Danger of Self Love: Re-Examining A Popular Myth*, gives this definition of self-love: "Self-love means simply that a person has a positive attitude about himself, feels good about himself. That is, when a person thinks about himself, he has a positive emotional response. Self-love, then, is basically an emotion or attitude." He goes on to explain that "Self-love theory begins with the assertion that large segments of society are suffering from a low self-image or lack of self-love. Often this is said to be a special problem among evangelical Christians because of the stress on the depravity of man in evangelical theology."[21]

Have you ever heard the phrase, "We must first learn how to love ourselves before we can love others?" This may sound good and even logical but it's definitely not sound doctrine.

TWO GREATEST COMMANDMENTS

In Matthew 22, a teacher of the law asks Jesus which is the greatest of the commandments? "And He said to him, 'You shall love the Lord your God with all your heart, and with all your soul, and with all your mind.' This is the great and foremost commandment. The second is like it, 'You shall love your neighbor as yourself'" (Matthew 22:37-39 NASB). Some interpret this as Jesus saying we must love ourselves, as if that's the problem. Rather, He is saying that it's a given that we already love ourselves.

Ephesians 5:28-29,33 (NASB), confirms this with words written under the inspiration of the Holy Spirit: "So husbands also ought to love their own wives as their own bodies. He who loves his own wife loves himself; for no one ever hated his own flesh, but nourishes and cherishes it, just as Christ also does the church . . . each husband is to love his own wife the same as himself."

The first, and greatest commandment, is a whole lot easier to do than the second because of all that God has done for us. The second becomes a lot more difficult if the statement were true that "large segments of society are suffering with a low self-image or lack of self-love." The truth is this is the only way we can love others the way Christ loves the Church, is by the love of Jesus flowing through us.

THE GREATEST OBSTACLE TO HOLINESS

Please, let me be clear, bashing Christians is not my intention while writing this. The burden I carry for this book comes from the first part of Hosea 4:6: "My people are destroyed for lack of knowledge." There are many who genuinely love the Lord, but they have not been given the full counsel of God.

FREE AT LAST

If this describes your condition, you may be asking the question, "What's the answer?" I want to share with you the secret to being set free from those besetting sins. It can be boiled down to only one word. There's only one thing you need to do, and it comes from none other than the Apostle Paul. He received it by revelation from the supreme authority, Jesus Christ. It is—die!

Neil Armstrong became the first person to walk on the moon on July 20, 1969. He famously said on that day, "That's one small step for man, one giant leap for mankind."

CULTURE OF DEATH

Four years later there was another momentous occasion when the Supreme Court of the United States decisions of Roe v. Wade and Doe v. Bolton decriminalized abortion nationwide in 1973. We've all probably heard the phrase "culture of death." That became the day that we, as a nation, took the giant leap from the culture of life to the culture of death.

Since that infamous decision, the sanctity of life has been under full assault by the one who is out "to seek, to kill, and to destroy." One of the main tenets of medical practitioners is, "First, do no harm." Now we have doctors actively promoting and taking part in euthanasia; the practice of ending the life of a patient to limit the patient's suffering.

On November 6, 2019, a letter of transmittal titled "Quality-Adjusted Life Years and the Devaluation of Life with Disability" was sent from the National Council on Disability to then president, Donald Trump. It was a five-report series on the intersection of disability and bioethics. Here is a quote from that letter which clearly sounds the alarm on society's devaluation of life. "In an effort to lower their healthcare costs, public and private health insurance providers have utilized the Quality Adjusted Life Year (QALY) to determine the cost-effectiveness of medications and treatment. QALYs place a lower value on treatments which extend the lives of people with chronic illnesses and disabilities. In this report, NCD found sufficient evidence of the discriminatory effects of QALYs to warrant concern, including concerns raised by bioethicists, patient rights groups, and disability rights advocates about the limited access to lifesaving medications for chronic illnesses in countries where QALYs are frequently used."[22]

The Bible says that Satan is an imitator of God with the verse, "No wonder, for even Satan disguises himself as an angel of light" (2 Corinthians 11:14 NASB). Despite this disguise, his goal is the exact opposite of God's. Satan's goal for all mankind is their death. John 10:10 (NASB) describes who Satan really is: "The thief comes only to steal and kill and destroy." The second part of that verse tell us what Christ's goal is for all mankind: "I came so that they would have life, and have it abundantly."

Satan is like a lot of politicians who author laws that create massive problems and then have the audacity to claim that they have the solution to resolve those issues. Let me give one example regarding the American family. Satan has practically destroyed the nuclear family—one with two parents and their children living in the same home. This has resulted in the destruction of millions of lives. He did this by inspiring politicians to create a welfare system for unwed mothers. In doing this he killed two birds with one stone, since he created a large voting block of those dependent on government subsidies and absolved men of their responsibility to raise the children they fathered. This single issue has also had a massive impact on the destruction of American culture as we have known it.

Let's start with the first issue: fatherless homes.

Here are the stats:

- 63 percent of youth suicides are from fatherless homes.
- 90 percent of all homeless and runaway children are from fatherless homes.
- 85 percent of all children who show behavior disorders come from fatherless homes.
- 80 percent of rapists with anger problems come from fatherless homes.
- 71 percent of all high school dropouts come from fatherless homes.
- 75 percent of all adolescent patients in chemical abuse centers come from fatherless homes.
- 70 percent of juveniles in state-operated institutions come from fatherless homes.
- 85 percent of all youths sitting in prisons grew up in a fatherless home.[23]

The second issue is unwed mothers. The United States Census Bureau reported, "About 7.6 million (11 percent) children lived with their mother only in 1968 compared to 15.3 million (21 percent) in 2020."[24] According to National Women's Law Center, "The poverty rate for families with children headed by unmarried mothers was 32.1 percent, compared to 14.3 percent for families with children headed by unmarried fathers and 5.9 percent of married couple families with children."[25]

Satan created the problem and now he offers his solution—death. He does this and claims that his motives are based on compassion. He tells women lies like these:

> "If you don't abort this baby your life as you know it will be destroyed."
>
> "Surely you want a better life for this child than what you can provide."
>
> "You are not emotionally ready to have this baby."
>
> "You struggle with handling the children you already have. If you have another one you will be overwhelmed."

What I'm about to say next may leave you scratching your head. Though Satan wants to "kill, steal, and destroy," and Christ wants to provide "life and that more abundantly," they both arrive at their goal through the "culture of death."

Although I have used the same phrase for both, Satan's is a culture of death to death (eternal death). Jesus's is a culture of death to life (eternal life). Jesus said that in order for us to live we must first die, die to self. Jesus instituted the New Covenant as a covenant of death. Jesus died in our place so that we might live. Jesus, shortly after raising Lazarus from the dead, and in anticipation of His approaching death, declared this culture of death when He said, "Truly, truly I say to you, unless a grain of wheat falls into the earth and dies, it remains alone" (John 12:24 NASB).

I imagine that most of you right now are experiencing the same emotional reaction that I am as I write this. It makes me uncomfortable to present a biblical truth and liken it to the phrase "culture of death." This reminds me of rubbing a cat's fur the wrong way. It can make them extremely uncomfortable, and some cats may even react aggressively. You may even be feeling the need to react aggressively as you read this.

My purpose in doing it is to jolt the reader into realizing that the Church has, for the most part, abandoned the message that Jesus preached. I love the way the AMPC Bible expands on this truth: "And He said to all, If any person wills to come after Me, let him deny himself [disown himself, forget, lose sight of himself and his own interests, refuse and give up himself] and take up his cross daily and follow Me [cleave steadfastly to Me, conform wholly to My example in living and, if need be, in dying also]." The cross Jesus took up led to his death in order that we might live. We must take up His cross daily, thus embracing death to self, that He might live within us.

I want to drive this point home. The Bible says that "On the testimony of two or three witnesses every matter shall be confirmed" (2 Corinthians 13:1 NASB). Here are some more witnesses in the Scriptures.

Hebrews 3:14 (NASB) says, "For we have become partakers of Christ." The Apostle Paul said it this way in Galatians: "I have been crucified with Christ [in Him I have shared His crucifixion]; it is no longer I who live, but Christ (the Messiah) lives in me" (Galatians 2:20). And "knowing this, that our old self was crucified with Him, in order that our body of sin might be done away with, so that we would no longer be slaves to sin" (Romans 6:6 NASB).

Many pastors and teachers need to take to heart the message Paul preached to the Corinthians. When Paul was in Corinth, he had one message: "For I determined to know nothing among you except Jesus Christ, and Him crucified. I also was with you in weakness and fear, and in great trembling, and my message and my preaching were not in persuasive words of wisdom, but in demonstration of the Spirit and of power, so that your faith would not rest on the wisdom of mankind, but on the power of God" (Corinthians 2:2 NASB).

WE HAVE NO RIGHTS

The United States Declaration of Independence has this phrase in it, "life, liberty, and the pursuit of happiness." This is considered an example of unalienable rights given to all humans by their Creator. Many have taken this to mean that people have the right to live their lives on their own terms and make their own choices.

These are the values that the world upholds but those are not the values in the Kingdom of God. I love what my pastor said, "Dead people have no rights." If we have truly died to self then we have no rights. With Christ living in us, He then calls the shots.

In First Samuel 8, when Samuel grew old, it says that he appointed his sons as Israel's leaders. It says that his sons were wicked men, so the elders of Israel told him to appoint a king over them. This upset Samuel but God told him that they hadn't rejected him as a person, but instead they had rejected God as their king. When the Israelites insisted that Samuel appoint a king over them, he explained how that would affect them (1 Samuel 8:10-17). He told them that whatever the king wanted the king would get. There wouldn't be a thing they could do about it. If he were a righteous and good king, the nation would prosper under his rule. If he wasn't, it was too bad, so sad.

Jesus is the King of Kings and the Lord of Lords—which is good news! Jesus is a righteous and just King and all that He does, He does them for our good. It has been said, "If Jesus is not Lord of all, he is not Lord at all." We do not have the right to live life on our own terms.

In order to live, to live victoriously over those besetting sins, you must die, die to self as it's said in this verse, "knowing this, that our old self was crucified with Him, in order that our body of sin might be done away with, so that we would no longer be slaves to sin; for the one who has died is freed from sin" (Romans 6:6-7 NASB).

Until we embrace that truth, and ruthlessly apply it to ourselves, we will never be free. We must crucify our desires, but they won't die easily. Jesus wants us to come to the end of ourselves. It is there that we surrender to Him and admit that we can't do it. We will then hear Him say to us what He said to Paul: "And He has said to me, 'My grace is sufficient for you, for power is perfected in weakness'" (2 Corinthians 12:9 NASB).

THE END OF SELF

The testimony of how I came to the Lord is how I learned the truth that God wants us to come to the end of ourselves. My dad was an Assemblies of God minister while also being a career man in the Army. I gave my heart to the Lord when I was around 7 or 8, but in my early teens I rebelled against what my parents taught me and ended up on the wrong path. I began to smoke and became addicted to cigarettes. I remember reading that the addiction to cigarettes is stronger than being addicted to cocaine. I still don't know if that is true or not, but one thing I do know, I couldn't beat the addiction to cigarettes in the strength of my own willpower.

Back in that day, if you smoked, we were told in the churches we attended that you were going straight to hell. Many years later, our pastor at the time, John Lindell, said, "I don't know that you will go to hell, but it will sure smell like you've been there."

Even though I was rebellious, if you lived under my parents' roof, you went to church every time the doors were open. There were times when the messages preached would bring me under such great conviction that I would go forward and leave a puddle of tears on the altar. I would resolve to quit smoking and throw my cigarettes away. But I would find myself the very next day looking for the nearest cigarette machine.

As I grew older it got to the point that I would sit in the back of the church, and when the preacher started preaching, I would slip out the back, go to the nearest Pizza Hut, smoke a cigarette and drink a Dr. Pepper. During this time, I was a miserable sinner. One night, the week of Thanksgiving in 1971, I didn't leave when the preacher started preaching. Even though I can't tell you what the message was, I can sure tell you that the Holy Spirit was doing a number on me.

When the pastor gave the invitation to come forward to receive Christ, he said that if it makes it easier, ask the person sitting next to you to go with you. So I did. I left the usual puddle of tears on the altar, but this time I did something different. I came to the end of myself. I confessed to the Lord that I loved smoking and I couldn't quit on my own. I had tried too many times and failed. I told the Lord that if He would deliver me from my addiction to cigarettes, I would serve him.

THE GREATEST OBSTACLE TO HOLINESS

That's the night this Scripture became real to me: "So if the Son sets you free, you really will be free" (John 8:36 NASB). From that moment on I lost my desire to smoke. I never smoked another cigarette after that.

At the time, I worked at a Coca-Cola plant in Lawton, Oklahoma. Unlike today, people who smoked in the 70s could smoke almost anywhere. So, the next day when I went into the breakroom and sat down by a guy smoking a cigarette, I couldn't even smell the smoke. That continued for the next three days. God had taken my sense of smell away for cigarettes for three days so that I wouldn't be tempted.

Now, there may be ministers who will be offended by what I say next and yet I feel compelled to say it. Many ministers base their messages on felt needs. Each week they think about needs that their congregation may be dealing with, such as depression, fear, and anxiety caused by current events (either nationally or world-wide), or the need for wisdom in making decisions about marriage, children, work, etc.

I'm not saying that this is wrong in and of itself. If ever there was a place to find help in addressing these problems, it's the Bible. There is definitely a need for pastors to address these issues from a biblical perspective. However, the problem is that these types of messages still have us focused on ourselves.

I cannot begin to tell you the many times I've listened to ministers of the Gospel of Jesus Christ in absolute amazement and awe; how they so eloquently and clearly preached messages addressing major concerns and issues of the day. But it is my firm conviction that until the Church of Jesus Christ focuses on this message above all others, Jesus Christ and Him crucified, many believers will continue to live defeated lives.

CHAPTER 7

DEFINING DEVIANCY DOWNWARD

"If you can sin and not weep over it, you are an heir to hell. If you can go into sin, and afterwards feel satisfied to have done so, then you are on the road to destruction. If there are no prickings of conscience, no inward torments, no bleeding wounds; if you have no throbs and heavings of a bosom that cannot rest; if your soul never feels filled with wormwood and gall when you know you have done evil, you are no child of God."

—Charles Spurgeon

*B*efore I get into the cost of discipleship, I feel the need to address what some have referred to as hyper-grace. If you are familiar with twentieth century church history, then you have heard talk about Christian legalism. Here, holiness was defined as not "engaging in social practices perceived as contrary to a Christian witness, such as gambling, dancing, consuming alcohol, enjoying secular entertainment, or wearing immodest clothing."[26]

I believe the pendulum has swung from an emphasis on holiness in the mid-twentieth century church, which was inordinately focused on outward appearance and actions rather than the condition of the heart, to the preeminence of grace. So much so, that the idea is conveyed that it doesn't really matter very much how we live—God will forgive. Couple that with a common phrase heard in churches today, "When you receive Jesus as your Savior He forgives your past, present, and future sins, and there isn't anyone that can snatch you from his hand."

I'm convinced that this is a recipe for disaster in the life of the Church when it's not coupled with sound doctrinal teaching on living a holy life. I can't tell you how many times I've heard Christians say, "Well, I know I'm going to sin today, but thank God for His wonderful grace." This is fatalism at its worst. Not only is that mindset fatalistic but it can foster an attitude that minimizes sin.

That's just what Satan wants us to do. A perfect example of how Satan does this is seen in the movie industry in America spanning the last 100 years. It's called desensitization. In 1939 the movie *Gone With the Wind*[27] came out. It had one profanity, and it was so scandalous that it cost the movie makers a hefty fine of 5,000 dollars, which was a lot at that time. That word that was used has now become so innocuous that I've heard it used at a Bible study and at a Men's Breakfast at church.

Over the years the movie industry and TV shows kept pushing the boundaries to the point that nothing is sacrosanct, unless it's politically incorrect. Of course, it then began to seep into the television industry where we now have homosexuals kissing in TV commercials, and vulgarity is so commonplace that it seems to me that movies or TV shows are required to use God's name as a curse word.

In order to justify going to movies or watching TV programs that are filled with vulgarity, I've heard Christians often say, "That's just the way it is in society. We can't avoid it at work, at school, during sporting events, etc. Sinners are going to do what sinners are going to do."

At the Last Supper, part of Jesus's prayer for the disciples was, "I am not asking You to take them out of the world, but to keep them away from the evil one" (John 17:15 NASB). Because we are in this world there are some things that we can't avoid. But how can the Father keep us from evil when we choose to take part in what the world offers?

You may have seen videos of people throwing trash out of their car windows and someone picking it up only to throw it back into the offender's car. I would personally recommend against that nowadays because you might get shot. That would naturally bother most people who saw something like that. There have been such strong anti-littering campaigns that it would stir strong feelings of anger in most of us.

VISUALIZATION

As I mentioned earlier, I not only love playing golf, but I also love watching it, though mostly on TV. Many professional golfers receive training from sports psychologists. Before hitting their drive off of the tee box, they are taught to stand behind the ball and visualize themselves hitting it perfectly down the fairway. Some golfers will actually close their eyes while doing this. I've personally tried my own visualization technique when playing golf, but it hasn't worked for me yet.

I think everyone can visualize what I'm about to ask next. The Bible teaches that those who have accepted Christ as their Savior are a temple of the Holy Spirit. "Or do you not know that your body is a temple of the Holy Spirit within you, whom you have from God, and that you are not your own? For you have been bought for a price: therefore glorify God in your body" (1 Corinthians 6:19-20 NASB). Because we are in this world, we experience the world throwing trash around us from time to time. We can't avoid it.

So this is what I want you to do. Visualize opening the top of your head and dumping a trash can filled with filthy, repulsive trash, represented by the entertainment we watch and listen to, into the temple where the Holy Spirit dwells. Wouldn't you agree that's a pretty repulsive picture and certainly not what we want to subject God, the Holy Spirit to?

Sometimes the world litters our lives with images and language that we can't avoid. However, it's another thing entirely when we intentionally open ourselves up and allow the world to dump their filth into us.

DEFINING DEVIANCY DOWNWARD

It used to be that our leaders in government would consider it a major *faux pas* to use profanity in a speech to the public. It's not so much anymore. This is from *The New York Post, Letters to the Editor* that's dated June 25, 2024: "Rep. Alexandria Ocasio-Cortez danced to a Cardi B song with lyrics degrading women. Rep. Jamaal Bowman then got up and used the vilest language imaginable.... With leaders like this, it's no wonder our kids think nothing about using this kind of language and acting inappropriately."[28] Lately, Democrats have begun to embrace combative, profanity-laced language to combat Trump.

CALLING SIN, SIN

Has the Church been immune to desensitization? Not at all. Referring back to a question I asked earlier, but now on a different topic: when was the last time your minister preached a hard hitting, no holds barred sermon on the topic of sin?

To follow this thought, this is what God told Ezekiel to do: "This is what God, the Master, says: Clap your hands, stamp your feet, yell out, 'No, no, no!' because of all the evil obscenities rife in Israel" (Ezekiel 6:11 MSG).

God told Isaiah, "Cry loudly, do not hold back; Raise your voice like a trumpet, and declare to My people their wrongdoing, and to the house of Jacob their sins" (Isaiah 58:1 NASB).

The Apostle Paul preached against sin to those in Galatia: "It is obvious what kind of life develops out of trying to get your own way all the time: repetitive, loveless, cheap sex; a stinking accumulation of mental and emotional garbage; frenzied and joyless grabs for happiness; trinket gods; magic-show religion; paranoid loneliness;

cutthroat competition; all-consuming-yet-never-satisfied wants; a brutal temper; an impotence to love or be loved; divided homes and divided lives; small-minded and lopsided pursuits; the vicious habit of depersonalizing everyone into a rival; uncontrolled and uncontrollable addictions; ugly parodies of community. I could go on" (Galatians 5:19-21 MSG).

He preached against sin to those in Colossae: "So kill (deaden, deprive of power) the evil desire lurking in your members [those animal impulses and all that is earthly in you that is employed in sin]: sexual vice, impurity, sensual appetites, unholy desires, and all greed and covetousness, for that is idolatry (the deifying of self and other created things instead of God). It is on account of these [very sins] that the [holy] anger of God is ever coming upon the sons of disobedience (those who are obstinately opposed to the divine will)" (Colossians 3:5-6 MSG).

He also preached to those in Corinth: "Or do you not know that the unrighteous will not inherit the kingdom of God? Do not be deceived; neither the sexually immoral, nor idolaters, nor adulterers, nor homosexuals, nor thieves, nor the greedy, nor those habitually drunk, nor verbal abusers, nor swindlers, will inherit the kingdom of God" (1 Corinthians 6:9 NASB).

LABOR INTENSIVE

It is true that salvation is given freely to us in Christ Jesus. However, the problem in the Church today is that many think that because we are saved by grace alone, through faith alone, and in Christ alone, that nothing else is required of us. This couldn't be further from the truth. Paul said it this way: "work out your own salvation with fear and trembling" (Philippians 2:12 NASB).

In 2 Samuel 24, when King David numbered the people, he sinned against God. "But when it was all done, David was overwhelmed with guilt because he had counted the people, replacing trust with statistics" (2 Samuel 24:10 MSG). God sent the prophet Gad to tell David that he had one of three choices. After Gad told him the three choices available, David told Gad, "They're all terrible! But I'd rather be punished by God, whose mercy is great, than fall into human hands" (2 Samuel 24:14 MSG). So God chose an angel to send three days of pestilence upon the land and at the end of the third day (the appointed time), 70,000 Israelites had died.

What's amazing is that David was able to see the angel. When David saw the angel poised to destroy Jerusalem, he cried out to God to spare the people because it wasn't their fault, it was his. "Please! I'm the one who sinned; I, the shepherd, did the wrong. But these sheep, what did they do wrong? Punish me and my family, not them" (2 Samuel 24:17 MSG). The prophet Gad then came to David and told him to erect an altar to the Lord. In other words, God required a sacrifice from David.

When the Bible says, "the appointed time," it is possibly referring to the time of the evening sacrifice. The angel of the Lord was standing by the threshing floor of Araunah, so, David went up to Araunah and offered to buy his threshing floor and oxen to sacrifice to the Lord.

Araunah offered to freely give him everything, but David said no. As a result of this story, we have one of David's most famous sayings. "No, but I will certainly buy it from you for a price; for I will not offer burnt offerings to the Lord my God that cost me nothing" (2 Samuel 24:24 NASB).

I left something out that was mentioned earlier because I want you to remember it. Before David went up and offered to purchase Araunah's property at a fair price, it said this back in 2 Samuel 24:16 (NASB): "And when the angel stretched out his hand upon Jerusalem to destroy it, the Lord relented of the evil *and* reversed His judgment and said to the destroying angel, 'It is enough; now stay your hand.'"

David was commanded to offer up a sacrifice to God after God had already stopped His judgment on Israel. The cost of the sacrifice came after the judgment was already suspended. In that same way, what costs us in the service of the Lord comes only after His grace has been extended to us and judgment against our sin has been stopped.

As someone has so aptly noted, in all of Paul's letters, excluding Hebrews if you are one of those who believe Paul was the author, he greets his readers with the phrase "Grace and peace to you. . . ." Grace always comes before peace. You will not experience God's peace without first experiencing His grace.

In the same way grace always comes before works.

CHAPTER 8

WHAT'S IN A NAME? SOMETIMES EVERYTHING

"Truly, truly I say to you, if you ask the Father for anything in My name, He will give it to you."

—JOHN 16:23

Why do we obey God? Is it because we fear His judgment, of spending eternity in hell? Or is it because we love him, and desire to bring honor and glory to His name?

Here's another way of phrasing these questions: How much does God hate sin and want His children to honor, respect, and revere His name? For us, this is where the rubber meets the road. Do we hate sin? We are essentially saying the same thing when we ask the question; how much do we honor, respect, and revere the name of the Lord?

As I mentioned earlier, I believe today's Church has lost, to a large extent, the reverence, respect, and honor that should be given to the great name of our God and Savior, Jesus Christ. And, in so doing, we are profaning the holy name of God. "Neither shall you profane My holy name [applying it to an idol or treating it with irreverence or contempt or as a byword]" (Leviticus 22:32). We also profane Christ's holy name by calling ourselves Christians while living no differently than the world. By doing so, we drag His name through the mud.

Did you know that one of the names of God is "Jealous?" "For you shall not worship any other god, because the Lord, whose name is Jealous, is a jealous God" (Exodus 34:14 NASB).

Most of us think of jealousy in a negative sense. The definition of jealous can be understood as "feeling or showing envy of someone, of others achievements and advantages." It can also be the "feeling or showing suspicion of someone's unfaithfulness in a relationship." And lastly, I think it's applicable to this verse, "fiercely protective or vigilant of one's rights or possessions."

When we think of God as a jealous God, it's certainly not because He's feeling envious of someone's achievements. I bet you were smiling as you read that, because that's unquestionably not the definition when applying it to God. We're talking about the same God who created everything out of nothing.

WHAT'S IN A NAME? SOMETIMES EVERYTHING

It's laughable to think He is suspicious of someone's faithfulness. He knows everything. You're either faithful or you're not, and He knows. What He is, is fiercely protective and vigilant when it comes to His Name.

"In Jewish thought, a name is not merely an arbitrary designation, a random combination of sounds. The name conveys the nature and essence of the thing named. It represents the history and reputation of the being named. This is not as strange or unfamiliar a concept as it may seem at first glance. In English, we often refer to a person's reputation as his 'good name.' When a company is sold, one thing that may be sold is the company's 'good will,' that is, the right to use the company's name. The Hebrew concept of a name is very similar to these ideas."[29]

I would like to ask you a question. How important is your reputation or name to you? Another way to ask this question is how do you want people to think of you when someone mentions your name? Here's another question. Have you ever had someone in your family do or say something that has had a negative impact on your family's name? We've all heard of the "black sheep of the family." Maybe that's you. Does your family's name come with a reputation? Is it good or bad?

Have you ever asked the question, "Isn't that so-and-so's son or daughter?" Was it because of their parents' reputation or because of their child's reputation that they are talked about in a certain way? In many cultures the honor of the family name is paramount. We've all heard of honor killings. Sadly, most of these have to do with women.

In an online article in *Forbes* magazine that's dated July 10, 2018, Avery Blank, the Senior Contributor writes, "What's in a name? A lot. Your name and how you use your name influences how you are perceived. And like it or not, perception is everything. In a fast and information-overloaded world, people make conclusions quickly and can overlook your value if you don't present yourself properly." Later on in the article she writes, "Sometimes authority should be worn lightly," like in nonbusiness situations. "But sometimes it should be brandished like a torch," she goes on to say."[30]

In Isaiah 42:8 (NASB), God through the prophet Isaiah declares, "I am the Lord, that is My name; I will not give My glory to another, Nor My praise to idols...." In his book *God's Devil*, Erwin Lutzer wrote, "The higher Lucifer aspired to ascend, the further he would of necessity fall. Did he misjudge God, thinking that His love would eclipse any possibility of stern judgment? We do not know, of course, but keep in mind that Lucifer had only seen God's perfect love. The concept of justice simply did not exist. As long as there was no disobedience in the universe, there was no need for the demonstration of God's anger. Lucifer did not foresee the lengths to which God is willing to go to preserve His honor."[31]

This brings us to the crux of the matter in a story recorded in Judges 19-20. It's not about the honor of the Levite, although I'm sure that's what motivated him; it's also not primarily about the honor of the nation of Israel either. That's the secondary point, but it is related to the primary focus of this passage in the Bible. It's about the honor of God's Name. And this is the burden that God has laid upon my heart.

My opinion is that the American Church in particular has, for the most part, lost the reverence and awe of the Name of God. Borrowing from Lutzer's quote above, I don't believe American believers are able to "foresee the lengths to which God is willing to go to preserve His honor."

WHAT'S IN A NAME? SOMETIMES EVERYTHING

When it comes to honoring God, Muslims put us to shame, even when they are just honoring the name of their prophet, Muhammad. In September of 1988, Salman Rushdie published his novel *The Satanic Verses* which caused immediate controversy in the Islamic world. On February 14, 1989, Ayatollah Khomeini, the Supreme leader of Iran, called for a fatwa, ordering Rushdie's execution.

I am in no way suggesting that Christians should respond this way when God's name is used in vain. That would be contrary to the Gospel of Jesus Christ. What I am stressing is the importance of a name and the honor attached to it in many cultures, especially in the Middle East.

Another example of how the Jews revered the name of God is revealed in the rules and procedures the Jewish scribes had to follow while creating copies of the Torah; and later on in other books in the Hebrew Bible. Here was the rule they had to follow when writing the name of God. "They must wipe the pen and wash their entire bodies before writing the most Holy Name of God, YHVH, and after every time they wrote it. Also, before they would write the most Holy Name of God, they would wash their hands seven times."[32]

To us in the western world this seems extreme. Especially in today's church culture in America, and many other places around the world, where everything is so casual now. Do I wish things were different? Yes. You might ask why and you might even say, "Don't be so uptight" or ask, "What's the big deal?" I think it's a sign of respect.

What I'm speaking to has to do with mindset and what comes to mind now is the broken window's theory. Criminologists George L. Kelling and James Q. Wilson authored an article for *The Atlantic*. "The idea [is] that once disorder begins, it doesn't matter what the neighborhood is, things can begin to get out of control."

In the article, Kelling and Wilson suggested that a broken window or other visible signs of disorder or decay—think loitering, graffiti, prostitution, or drug use—can send the signal that a neighborhood is uncared for. So, they thought if police departments addressed those problems, maybe the bigger crimes wouldn't happen.[33]

The article goes on to mention the most famous instance of this being implemented was by Rudy Giuliani, when he won the election for New York City mayor in 1993 by promising to reduce crime and clean up the streets. Crime fell, the murder rate plummeted, and Giuliani easily won re-election again in 1997.

All I'm suggesting is when it comes to attending church, the importance of our mindset is necessary. The great golfer, Arnold Palmer, once said, "Golf is a game of inches. The most important are the six inches between your ears."

I remember a time in America when Sunday was considered the most important day of the week. Many states had blue laws, which were also known as Sunday laws. The purpose of these were to restrict or ban some, or all, Sunday activities in particular, to promote the observance of a day that's for worship or rest. It was unheard of when I was growing up that sports for children and teens were scheduled on Sundays. I don't remember playing a baseball game or having baseball practice on Wednesdays because that was recognized as a church night back then. It could be that they did, but my parents wouldn't have given priority to baseball practice or a game over church. We've come a long way from those times.

I would like to borrow Mr. Palmer's quote with minor changes: When it comes to attending church and worshipping, it's a matter of inches as well. The most important is the distance between the brain (mind) and the heart. How do we approach church and what is our mindset when we worship God? Is it pretty much just another day when we go to be entertained, have a great time, and fulfill our spiritual obligation? Or is it a time when we come to sit and worship at the feet of the Creator. Much of what we get out of anything is what we do in preparation.

In the Song of Solomon 2:15 (MSG) it says, "Then you must protect me from the foxes, foxes on the prowl, foxes who would like nothing better than to get into our flowering garden." I like the commentary provided by gotquestions.org: "It might seem strange that, in the middle of a romantic, tender conversation, the matter of a fox hunt should arise. As with much of the imagery in this beautiful poem, the foxes are symbolic.

"Solomon's readers considered foxes to be destructive animals that could destroy valuable vineyards (cf. Judges 15:4; Psalm 63:10; Ezekiel 13:4). As the Shulammite and her beloved verbalize their love for each other, we are suddenly confronted with the need to catch the foxes that spoil the vines. If the blossoming vineyard spreading its fragrance (Song of Solomon 2:13) refers to the growing romance between the couple, then the foxes of verse 15 represent potential problems that could damage the relationship prior to the marriage (which takes place in chapter 5). The command is 'Take preventative measures to protect this love from anything that could harm it.'"[34]

My wife likes to remind me of what our pastor said when he married us: "Garry, you've got to keep doing the things that you did to win her love. Don't stop doing them once you get married." It's the little things that we do or don't do (broken windows) that can ruin our relationship with the Lord. Do you remember what it was like when you first gave your heart to the Lord? Hopefully, you were excited about going to church. You never wanted to miss a service, and you made sure to show up early. You loved entering into worship, and you hung on to every word the pastor said. Have things changed over time?

Here are some reasons we don't go to church: "It's raining cats and dogs, and I don't want to step in a poodle;" "it's so cold, I actually saw a gangsta pull his pants up;" "we need family time and, some weeks we get just one day;" "we don't get much from the pastor's messages;" "the lake is calling;" or "I'm just too tired." The first two are silly jokes but, in reality, aren't they all just excuses?

I'm reminded of a song the Righteous Brothers used to sing called *You've Lost That Lovin' Feelin*. The lyrics apply to many in the Church today.

LOVING BY EXAMPLE

My dad showed me and my two brothers how to treat a woman by how he treated our mom. She always came first, even before us kids. He always treated her with respect and one of the ways he did that was by taking care of his appearance. He was always well groomed when out in public to not embarrass her. He would also never allow us kids to disrespect or talk back to her. He always opened the door for her when entering a building and let her walk through first. He opened the car door for her and when walking down the street he would always be between her and the traffic in case he needed to protect her from an accident. He wanted to outlive her because he always wanted to be there to protect and provide for her.

Unfortunately for him, the Lord called him home first. He died of cancer, and it really bothered him when he realized he would be going first. He did all of these things, not because he had too, but because he

WHAT'S IN A NAME? SOMETIMES EVERYTHING

loved her to his very last breath. Because of his example, I try to treat my wife in the same way to show my respect and love for her in the ways my father showed my mother his.

In that same way, my mother showed my sister how to treat a man by how she treated our dad. My dad was a career military man, and my mom would shine his brass and shoes for him. It was not because he asked her too, but because she loved him. She ironed his clothes often and when it came to cooking, what he wanted to eat was considered first. She never showed him disrespect and always spoke well about him to others.

With both my mom and my dad, we kids never felt unloved or neglected because they put each other first. They showed their love for us in so many other ways. Oftentimes, they were sacrificing their own needs to make sure ours were met. In this day of no-fault divorce, where so many children are scarred for life when their parents get divorced, we had the great comfort of knowing that they were committed to each other no matter how difficult things got.

Luke 14:26 (AMPC) says, "If anyone comes to Me and does not hate his [own] father and mother [in the sense of indifference to or relative disregard for them in comparison with his attitude toward God] and [likewise] his wife and children and brothers and sisters—[yes] and even his own life also, he cannot be my disciple." This is a strong statement that I think most of us haven't really considered. The Lord didn't say that we won't be a good disciple, instead He said we cannot be His disciple. Is it because He won't let us be His disciple that we chose not to serve or is it because following Him, and the life he calls us to live, demands everything of us?

Our attitude (mindset), and love for the Lord is paramount to our discipleship. Both of these attributes, if regarded correctly, will have a tremendous influence on who God is to us; it's in how we serve and worship him, and why we live the way we live.

Oxford Dictionary defines attitude as, "A settled way of thinking or feeling about someone or something, typically one that is reflected in a person's behavior." Mindset is defined by this same dictionary as: "The established set of attitudes held by someone."[35] The question then becomes, "What is our attitude and mindset when it comes to God?" Our behavior either affirms or betrays our attitude (mindset).

CHAPTER 9

WHAT'S AT STAKE? ETERNITY

"The stakes are too high for us to die with a small vision."

—Louie Giglio

It's a simple question and yet your response to it will be the most important answer you ever make. The subject is eternity, and the question of all questions is, "Where will you spend it?"

I base this question upon the absolute certainty that the Bible is truly the holy, infallible, inerrant, God-breathed, Word of God to mankind. Because this statement is true, it naturally follows that what the Bible has to say about eternity, and where you spend it, is of paramount importance.

The Bible says that when you were born, your physical body will eventually die but you will receive an immortal body that is indestructible, it will never die. You will live forever, for all eternity, and you will spend that eternity in one of two places—heaven or hell. The Bible also says that you have a choice where you will spend eternity, but that choice can only be made in this lifetime. At the moment your physical body dies your destiny will be forever decided. There won't be any do-overs, no second chances.

The Apostle Paul tells us in 2 Corinthians 5:6 (NASB) that "while we are at home in the body we are absent from the Lord." He then tells us in verse 8 that we "prefer rather to be absent from the body and to be at home with the Lord." Jesus affirmed this on the cross when He told the thief that "today" he would be with Him in paradise.

There may be some reading this that have been taught the doctrine of purgatory. "According to Rome, Christ's merit imputed to us is not enough to save; we must earn more merit of our own through the sacraments and other good works. Righteousness is infused into us (rather than being imputed to us)."[36]

"Salvation comes no other way; no other name has been or will be given to us by which we can be saved, only this one" (Acts 4:12 MSG). Here, Peter said, "no other name—only this one." That seems pretty exclusive to me. To claim that we need others to pray for us so that we may be cleansed in order to go to heaven is to declare that the gift of God, Jesus Christ, for our salvation was insufficient to cleanse us from all unrighteousness. Paul in Titus 3:5 (NASB), says, "not on the basis of deeds which we did in righteousness, but in accordance with His mercy."

Finally, Paul in Romans 4:5 (MSG) declares this: "But if you see that the job is too big for you, that it's something only God can do, and you trust him to do it—you could never do it for yourself no matter

WHAT'S AT STAKE? ETERNITY

how hard and long you worked—well, that trusting-him-to-do-it is what gets you set right with God, by God. Sheer gift."

One other claim made by the Catholic Church that I would like to address is found in 1 Corinthians 3:15. Here, they believe it tells us that any sins remaining in us must be cleansed by fire. I am indebted to this next website for the rebuttal to this claim. "The passage does not say that believers pass through the fire, but rather that a believer's works pass through the fire. 1 Corinthians 3:15 refers to the believer "escaping through the flames," not "being cleansed by the flames."[37]

The Bible, from beginning to end, Genesis to Revelation, is about one person, Jesus Christ. The most important person that has ever lived is Jesus, and He confirms the question "Where will you spend eternity" with the one He asked in Matthew 16:26: "For what good will it do a person if he gains the whole world, but forfeits his soul? Or what will a person give in exchange for his soul?"

The wisest man that ever lived according to the Bible, other than Jesus, is my second witness to the importance of this question. His name was Solomon, and this is his account in his own words.

> *"Oh, I did great things: built houses, planted vineyards, designed gardens and parks and planted a variety of fruit trees in them, made pools of water to irrigate the groves of trees. I bought slaves, male and female, who had children, giving me even more slaves; then I acquired large herds and flocks, larger than any before me in Jerusalem. I piled up silver and gold, loot from kings and kingdoms. I gathered a chorus of singers to entertain me with song, and—most exquisite of all pleasures— voluptuous maidens for my bed.*
>
> *"Oh, how I prospered! I left all my predecessors in Jerusalem far behind, left them behind in the dust. What's more, I kept a*

clear head through it all. Everything I wanted I took—I never said no to myself. I gave in to every impulse, held back nothing. I sucked the marrow of pleasure out of every task—my reward to myself for a hard day's work!

"Then I took a good look at everything I'd done, looked at all the sweat and hard work. But when I looked, I saw nothing but smoke. Smoke and spitting into the wind. There was nothing to any of it. Nothing."

—Ecclesiastes 2:4-11 MSG

If Solomon had been alive when Jesus asked the question "What shall it profit . . .?" he would have given the loudest amen to that question. The reason he would have done so reminds me of what someone has humorously said, "I've never seen a hearse pulling a U-Haul." You can't take anything physical with you. Later, in Ecclesiastes 2:18-19 (MSG), he says, "And I hated everything I'd accomplished and accumulated on this earth. I can't take it with me— no, I have to leave it to whoever comes after me. Whether they're worthy or worthless—and who's to tell?—they'll take over the earthly results of my intense thinking and hard work. Smoke."

The bitter truth of these verses is seen in 1 Kings 11:43, and in the following chapters, when Solomon's son, Rehoboam, ascended to the throne when his father died. The foolishness of Rehoboam was revealed within the first few weeks when most of Israel rejected Rehoboam as their king and chose Jeroboam to rule instead. Within five years most of what Solomon had worked so hard for was lost when Jerusalem and the temple were plundered by their enemies.

Solomon penned Ecclesiastes near the end of his life and, in Ecclesiastes 12:13 (MSG), it records some of his final words: "The last and final word is this: Fear God. Do what he tells you."

CHAPTER 10

WHAT'S AT STAKE? (PART 2): HEAVEN

"Hold the cross high so I can see it through the flames."

(Before being burned at the stake for her faith.)

—JOAN OF ARC

The psalmist said, "I will give thanks to You, because I am awesomely and wonderfully made; wonderful are Your works, and my soul knows it very well" (Psalm 139:14 NASB). As awesome as the human body is, the Bible teaches that when our body dies, as believers, we will experience a dimension much greater than what we have ever known here on this earth.

DRESSING GOD

The Apostle Paul gives us a glimpse of what it will be like in 1 Corinthians 15:40,42-44 (NASB), "There are also heavenly bodies and earthly bodies, but the glory of the heavenly is one, and the glory of the earthly is another. . . . So also, is the resurrection of the dead. It is sown a perishable body, it is raised an imperishable body; it is sown in dishonor, it is raised in glory; it is sown in weakness, it is raised in power; it is sown a natural body, it is raised a spiritual body. If there is a natural body, there is also a spiritual body."

If you want to get really excited about what our future bodies will be like, then stop and meditate on this. "Beloved, we are [even here and] now God's children; it is not yet disclosed (made clear) what we shall be [hereafter], but we know that when He comes and is manifested, we shall [as God's children] resemble and be like Him, for we shall see Him just as He [really] is" (1 John 3:2 AMPC).

Do you remember what John said in the Gospel of John 20:19 (MSG) after Jesus was raised from the dead? "Later on that day, the disciples had gathered together, but, fearful of the Jews, had locked all the doors in the house. Jesus entered, stood among them, and said, "Peace to you." Locked doors couldn't keep him out and if you believe that the angel rolled the stone from the entrance of the tomb so that Jesus could get out, then you need to change your thinking. The angel rolled the stone away so that everyone could see that the tomb was already empty.

You may have read the book by Don Piper, a Baptist minister, titled *90 Minutes in Heaven*. This is from the back cover: "He was driving a car that was crushed by a semi that crossed into his lane. Medical personnel said that he died instantly. While his body lay lifeless inside the ruins of his car, Piper experienced the glories of heaven, awed by its beauty and music." These were his words: "Everything I experienced was like a first-class buffet for the senses. I had never felt such powerful embraces or feasted my eyes on such beauty. Heaven's light and texture defy earthly eyes or explanation. Warm, radiant light engulfed me. As I looked around, I could hardly grasp the vivid, dazzling colors. Every hue and tone surpassed anything I had ever seen."[38] Our heavenly bodies and heaven itself will be beyond our wildest imaginations.

There are only two men in the Bible who had it said that they were loved by God. Daniel was told that he was greatly beloved (Daniel 9:23). This same Daniel that God spoke of so highly had a vision of Gabriel. When he did, he was so terrified he passed out.

John refers to himself in his gospel four times as the one Jesus loved (John 13:23, 19:26, 20:2, 21:7). John was with Jesus for three and a half years. But when John saw Jesus in His glorified body, he fell at His feet as if dead (Revelation 1:17).

These were just visions. Now, can you imagine what it will be like when we are actually in the presence of God? I don't think our natural perishable bodies could physically handle it. We will be overwhelmed by the glory and majesty that we will behold, and the awe, joy, and delight that will fill us. That's why we have to be raised with a powerful, imperishable, physical body.

WILL HEAVEN BE THE SAME FOR EVERYONE?

Heaven will be indescribably wonderful for everyone, just not the same for everyone. Jesus said in Revelation 22:12 (NASB), "Behold, I am coming quickly, and My reward is with Me, to reward each one as his work deserves."

DRESSING GOD

Let me describe two extremely different groups of people who will be in heaven. There will be people like the Apostle Paul, who in 2 Corinthians 11:24-27 (MSG), described what he went through as he fulfilled God's call on his life: "I've worked much harder, been jailed more often, beaten up more times than I can count, and at death's door time after time. I've been flogged five times with the Jews' thirty-nine lashes, beaten by Roman rods three times, pummeled with rocks once. I've been shipwrecked three times and immersed in the open sea for a night and a day. In hard traveling year in and year out, I've had to ford rivers, fend off robbers, struggle with friends, struggle with foes. I've been at risk in the city, at risk in the country, endangered by desert sun and sea storm, and betrayed by those I thought were my brothers. I've known drudgery and hard labor, many a long and lonely night without sleep, many a missed meal, blasted by the cold, naked to the weather."

There were many others, like Billy Graham, who were the means of millions coming to a saving faith in the Lord Jesus Christ. There were also multitudes of martyrs who died because of their faith in Jesus and their refusal to deny him.

On the opposite end of the scale, there will be others like the thief who died upon the cross next to Jesus. They lived like the devil until the last moments of their lives, but as they approached eternity, they realized the awfulness of their sin and their impending arrival in hell. At that moment they cried out to Jesus to forgive them and God, in His great mercy, did the unthinkable and forgave them. When viewed in that light, would it seem right for the latter group to receive the same rewards as the former?

Some of you when reading that last line may be thinking, *Hold on a second. What about the parable that Jesus told of the workers in*

WHAT'S AT STAKE? (PART 2): HEAVEN

the vineyard in Matthew 20? Workers that only worked an hour were paid the same amount as those who worked all day. The workers who worked all day began to grumble because they weren't paid more. The owner of the vineyard reminded them that they had agreed to work based on the amount he had said he would pay them. He paid them the agreed amount. He was not being unfair by being generous to those who only worked one hour.

In a similar manner, all who put their faith in Jesus Christ will receive the same promise of eternal life and heaven will be their home for all eternity, regardless of whether they lived for Him all of their lives or put their faith in Him with their dying breath. Such is the generosity of our God. The promise of eternal life is received by faith, not by works. Rewards, on the other hand, are based on our works done for Christ after we have put our faith in Him.

One of the attributes of God is that He is a God of justice. It is part of His character, which means He is always just. Also, He is omniscient and knows everything. Because of this, no one will ever be able to say He made a mistake. How just would it be of God to give the same reward to everyone, regardless of their works? Well, I have some great news for you. If, looking back at your past life, you don't see much that would merit rewards, then from this moment forward you can choose to change that.

There are some who believe that believers should not work in order to gain rewards, but Jesus had much to say about rewards that will be given us. Here are just a few passages: (Matthew 6:4,6, 10:41-42; Luke 6:23,35). Much is also written in the Old and New Testament about both the future rewards and the rewards we can receive while here on the earth (cf. Psalm 19:11, 62:12; Jeremiah 31:16; Proverbs

11:18, 13:13; 1 Corinthians 3:8, 9:24; Colossians 3:24; Hebrews 10:35; 2 John 1:8).

Proverbs 11:31 (MSG) says, "If good people barely make it, what's in store for the bad!" The big word here is the little word "if." We have all heard stories of people or specific groups of people, who seem to, or actually do, get away with anything; this includes murder, and they suffer no consequences for it.

Then there are others who obey the law, and are unjustly accused of wrongdoing, and are unfairly imprisoned. In Psalms, the writer Asaph was, in his own words, grieved and embittered; completely frustrated with the seeming injustice of evil doers. He writes, "Until I entered the sanctuary of God. Then I saw the whole picture: The slippery road you've put them on, with a final crash in a ditch of delusions. In the blink of an eye, disaster!" (Psalm 73:17-19 MSG).

There is a day coming when a just God will hand out just rewards to the righteous and the unrighteous. To the righteous, He said, "Do not store up for yourselves treasures on earth.... But store up for yourselves treasures in heaven.... For where your treasure is, there your heart will be also" (Matthew 6:19-21 NASB).

JUDGMENT SEAT OF CHRIST

For the believer, 2 Corinthians 5:10 says, "For we must all appear and be revealed as we are before the judgment seat of Christ, so that each one may receive [his pay] according to what he has done in the body, whether good or evil [considering what his purpose and motive have been, and what he has achieved, been busy with, and given himself and his attention to accomplishing]."

WHAT'S AT STAKE? (PART 2): HEAVEN

This is called the Judgment Seat of Christ, which is also referred to as the Bema Judgment. This judgment does not determine where we spend eternity since we will be with God forever. Instead, it determines how we spend eternity. As believers we have already been justified (as if we had never sinned), because the righteousness of Christ has been imputed to us. What Christ will be judging are the works we did while serving Him here on earth. Paul, in 1 Corinthians 3:13, speaks of this Day of Judgment, and about the works done in this present body that will be revealed for what they are, either good or bad.

If our motives were wrong or impure, to gain the praise of men and not for the glory of God, then they will be considered as wood, hay, and stubble; this will all be destroyed. Only those works done out of love for God and for the glory of God will remain; these are described as gold, silver, and costly stones.

In short, what will be judged are the works we did for Him while here on this earth. Our rewards, and loss of rewards will be based on those works done in His name. Just as it's said in this verse, "For we are His workmanship, created in Christ Jesus for good works, which God prepared beforehand so that we would walk in them" (Ephesians 2:10). The greatness of our rewards will not be based only on the number of our good works. It will also be based on the motives behind those good works, and our obedience to doing those works which God prepared in advance for us to do. Those rewards will be the difference we all experience in heaven.

There are many types of rewards mentioned in the Bible and these rewards are based on what God has called us to do. We may be inclined to think that we will never receive rewards as great as those people who have done great things in advancing the Kingdom of God.

In Romans 12:3, Paul says that we all have gifts that differ according to the grace given to us and each gift requires a different measure of faith.

In the Parable of the Talents (Matthew 25), the master called on his servants and entrusted his wealth to them. To one, he gave five talents, to another he gave two, and then to another, he gave one. Their rewards were based on their faithfulness in handling what their master gave them to do. I love what the master told the first two: "Well done, good and faithful slave. You were faithful with a few things, I will put you in charge of many things" (Matthew 25:21 NASB). God is a generous God, and His generosity will far exceed our expectations. His rewards will be based on our faithfulness to our giftings, no matter how great or small. There will be some in heaven who received greater giftings while here on earth, but were not as faithful as they should have been, thus their rewards won't be as great as they could've been.

Meanwhile, there will be others who received smaller giftings, but were faithful, so their reward will be greater.

CHAPTER 11

WHAT'S AT STAKE? (PART 3) – HELL

"Procrastination is the arrogant assumption that God owes you another opportunity to do what you had time to do."

—UNKNOWN

Here's a quote that we've all heard. It's the phrase "hope springs eternal," which comes from Alexander Pope's poem, *An Essay on Man*, from the eighteenth century. There are untold stories throughout history about people who have endured extreme hardship, indescribable pain, horrific suffering, and heartbreaking loss. And yet they held on because of one little word—hope! As long as they had hope, even just a smidgen of it, that their circumstances would eventually change, they were able to hold on.

Studies show that the most common reason that people commit suicide is because of depression. Severe pain and suffering can cause people to believe there's no hope of ever finding relief, which can lead to extreme depression. Once people lose hope, they no longer have any reason to live.

That leads me to a quote from Dante Alighieri's renowned epic poem, *Inferno*, "All hope abandon, ye who enter here." These are the words that greeted those who were entering hell. Let those words sink into your spirit. For those who end up in hell, all hope for their situation to change is gone forever. There are myriads of people who wouldn't take the chance of losing their hard-earned money through gambling, and yet they will gamble on where they will spend eternity by putting off the conviction of the Holy Spirit to repent.

Did you know that there is actually a club for procrastinators? In 1956 a man by the name of Les Waas, along with a few other men, came up with the idea for a club. It's called the "Procrastination Club of America" (PCA). Here's a quote about this organization: "It was the beginning of what must be the longest run of procrastination pranks ever perpetrated.... In 1966, a large group of PCA members took a bus hung with the banner 'Excursion to New York's World Fair.' That fair had actually closed a year and a half earlier—that is, unless they were heading for the 1939 fair; no one was entirely sure. Dutifully, the club members took snaps of the now defunct exhibits and empty venues."[39] Now that's a humorous view of procrastination.

Here is the opposite view of procrastination that is much more relevant to the subject of hell. It is from a quote by Charles Spurgeon.

WHAT'S AT STAKE? (PART 3) – HELL

"O unbelievers, I would not be in your place five minutes for all the world! As the Lord lives, there is but a step between you and hell! Only a breath, and you may be gone. If I were in your place, I should be afraid to eat a morsel of bread tonight, lest a crumb should go the wrong way, and by causing my death should land me in everlasting misery. One might be afraid to shut his eyes tonight as an unbeliever, lest, as he closed them on earth, he shut them forever to all light and hope."

NOT NOW

There may be some reading this who have not yet repented of your sins, and asked Jesus to save you, and to be Lord of your life. One of Satan's favorite strategies is to convince people that there's plenty of time to make that decision. You may feel, as you read this, the Holy Spirit's conviction to surrender your life to Christ. It may surprise you that Satan will suggest, "Sure, that's what you really need to do. Just not now." You may have something really fun planned for tonight or this coming weekend. If you make him Lord of your life, it will ruin your plans because you know your plans will not meet with Jesus's approval. Plus, He will buttress his argument with the lie, "Christians don't have any fun. So have your fun now." What you are hearing now is from Satan, and he is saying, "Wait until tomorrow. Or next week. Or next month. Or next year. You have plenty of time."

It's my earnest desire that what follows will awaken you to the gravity of your situation. You are on the brink of hell if you are without Christ, and you have no promise of tomorrow.

Consider these statistics:

World Death Rate

Deaths per Day: 170,790

Deaths per Hour: 7116

Deaths per minute: 119

Deaths per second: 1.98

The United States is number 3 in the world in deaths per day behind China and India with 8,341, which equates to 348 per hour. That comes to a grand total of 3,048,480 deaths in the United States in 2024.[40] Are you willing to risk spending an eternity in hell for another second, minute, or hour of pleasure?

HELL WON'T BE THE SAME FOR EVERYONE

Now, the same question we asked about heaven can be asked about hell. Will hell be the same for everyone? If so, people like Mao Zedong, founder of the Chinese Communist Party (responsible for 40 to 80 million deaths or more); Hitler, dictator of Germany, (blamed for 12 million concentration camp deaths and 30 million other deaths); Stalin, dictator of the Soviet Union (believed responsible for between 30 to 40 million "unnatural deaths;"[41] all quotes from *The Washington Post*); Pol Pot, leader of Cambodia (estimated 1.2 to 2.8 million—between 13-30 percent of the country's population at the time (*UCLA Newsroom*), deserve no greater punishment than anyone else in hell.[42]

God told the Israelites through Jeremiah that, "Your evil regime is fuel for my anger" (Jeremiah 21:12 MSG). The evils that we commit in this life, unless covered by the blood of Jesus Christ, will become the fuel of the fires of hell. Jesus told us to lay up treasures in heaven. Scripture tells us that those who do not repent are storing up fuel for the fires of hell in which they will burn for eternity.

Just as there is a judgment of the righteous, there will be a judgment of the sinners as well, so you can be confident that they will get their just desserts. "Then I saw a great white throne and Him who sat upon it, from whose presence earth and heaven fled, and no place was found for them. And I saw the dead, the great and the small, standing before the throne, and books were opened; and another book was opened, which is the book of life; and the dead were judged from the things which were written in the books, **according to their deeds.** . . . And if anyone's name was not found written in the book of life, he was thrown into the lake of fire" (Revelation 20:11-12, 15, NASB, emphasis mine). During this judgment, the God of all the earth will make everything right. In fact, all the injustices in the history of mankind will be made right.

WHAT ABOUT HELL?

Hell will be far worse than anything anyone could conjure up in their wildest imaginations. There has never been another person on earth that had more knowledge of hell than Jesus. In fact, Jesus spoke of hell more than anyone else in the Bible. There are many who believe in heaven, but these same people don't believe in hell. Or, if they do believe in hell, they hold on to the theology of "annihilationism;" that all damned humans and fallen angels, including Satan, will be totally destroyed, and their consciousness extinguished rather than suffering forever.

Jesus used the same Greek word for eternal when speaking of heaven as he did when speaking of hell. In Matthew 25 Jesus said that on the day of judgment everyone would be divided into two groups—sheep and goats. In verse 46 of that same chapter, He said, "These will go away into eternal punishment, but the righteous into eternal life" (Matthew 25:46 NASB).

DARKNESS

Let me share with you some of what the Bible has to say about hell. Some people joke that if they end up in hell, they will be there with all their friends. That may be true, but it won't be a party. Not only that, but even if they are there, they would never see them because hell is a place of total darkness (Matthew 8:12, 25:30; Jude 1:13). Matthew speaks of hell as a place of outer darkness where there will be weeping and gnashing of teeth (Matthew 22:13). The Apostle John, in Revelation 16:10, speaks of people being plunged into a darkness that is so great that they gnaw their tongues in agony.

Have you ever been in so much pain that if you suddenly experience new pain, it's a relief because it distracts you somewhat from the old pain? Could that be why they gnaw their tongues?

INDESCRIBABLE PAIN AND THIRST

Jesus tells the story of the rich man and Lazarus in Luke 16. The rich man asks Abraham to send Lazarus "to dip the tip of his finger in water and cool my tongue, because I am in agony in this fire" (Luke 16:24 NASB).

WHAT'S AT STAKE? (PART 3) – HELL

If you've ever suffered a burn, just imagine that pain you experienced, only exponentially greater in magnitude. Now imagine that pain along with a heat so oppressive that you struggle for every breath. Combine that with what Paul describes as "the stench from a rotting corpse" (2 Corinthians 2:16 MSG). Revelation 14:10 speaks of being tormented with burning sulfur. So, as you are struggling to breathe your senses are assaulted with the most horrific smell imaginable. Someone has said that the rich man is still waiting for that drop of water on his tongue.

NO REST

You may be saying at this point, "Okay, okay, enough, enough!" But I must continue. "And the smoke of their torment ascends forever and ever; they have no rest day and night" (Revelation 14:11 NASB). There is no rest for all eternity for those who end up in hell.

Let me see if I can summarize what the experience will be for those consigned to this awful place for all eternity.

You will be in a place where it is so dark that you gnaw your tongue in pain, your skin will be on fire, you will have an insatiable thirst that will never be relieved, you'll be struggling to breathe, while only succeeding to breathe in the most horrible of smells. Now, on top of all that, you are beyond exhaustion, always moving, never stopping, never resting, and, in the darkness, you bump into other people.

The pain is bad enough when you have an exposed nerve in a tooth with nothing touching it. Bite down on something with that tooth and what happens? The pain skyrockets! Since your skin is already on fire, you think it can't get any worse, but then you bump into something, or someone, unexpectedly in total darkness and it too, becomes exponentially worse. Once you experience that, you now have this overwhelming fear of it happening again. So, now imagine this fear, tension, and stress to keep maxing out forever.

DEAFENING NOISE NON-STOP

The best way to describe the next source of suffering in hell is to refer to the worship of the saints that are gathered around the throne of God in heaven. "After that I heard what sounded like the shout of a vast throng, like the boom of many pounding waves, and like the roar of terrific *and* mighty peals of thunder, exclaiming, Hallelujah (praise the Lord)! For now, the Lord our God the Omnipotent (the All-Ruler) reigns (Revelation 19:6)!" What an incredible experience that will be.

Now I know that this doesn't appeal to some of you around my age. The common refrain in churches nowadays from those of my generation is that the music is too loud! It will no longer bother us in our resurrected bodies. When I was younger, I loved loud cars and motorcycles, and especially loud music. If you've ever been to a concert, you can feel the bass in your chest. "That's because your chest is a resonant chamber, which means that it vibrates in response to vibrations at its natural frequency. When you hear a low bass tone, the chest vibrates because it matches this body part's own natural frequency."[43] Despite my age, I still like my music loud, but not for long periods of time.

Have you ever been at the point of exhaustion and your nerves were on edge? What was it that you wanted most at that time? One thing you wanted most at this point was some peace and quiet. However, that's never going to happen in hell. Can you imagine how loud the screams of millions of people in pain sound? Especially those with voices raised in hate, rage, and anger. The air will be filled with curses, and it never ends.

THE WORST SUFFERING OF ALL

Remember the quote above by Don Piper about heaven? "Everything I experienced was like a first-class buffet for the senses. I had never felt such powerful embraces or feasted my eyes on such beauty."

Hell will be just the opposite of heaven. You will want to die, but because you have an immortal body it will never, never, never happen. "None sink so far into hell as those who come nearest heaven, because they fall from the greatest of heights," as said by William Gurnall.

All this time I've been talking about physical pain. There is another pain that will be experienced in Hell and that is mental anguish, which will drive you insane. Your memory will cause the worst of it because memories will be horrific in hell. Hell is an eternity of regret. I believe that those who are condemned to hell for eternity will have the same enhanced senses that those in heaven will experience.

"The human brain may be able to hold as much information in its memory as is contained on the entire Internet, new research suggests. Researchers discovered that, unlike a classical computer that codes information as 0s and 1s, a brain cell uses twenty-six different ways to code its "bits." They calculated that the brain could store one petabyte (or a quadrillion bytes) of information.

"This is a real bombshell in the field of neuroscience," Terry Sejnowski, a biologist at the Salk Institute in La Jolla, California, said in a statement. "Our new measurements of the brain's memory capacity increase conservative estimates by a factor of 10."[44]

Those believers who chose to serve two gods—God and themselves—will remember every sermon they ever heard, every worship song they ever sang, every bit of joy and delight they felt in the presence of the Lord, and every feeling of the conviction from the Holy Spirit calling them to complete surrender to the Lordship of Jesus Christ.

We have all done things that we regret. Even as you are reading this, you may be thinking of something in your past that fills you with regret. Regret comes with a wish. You wish you could have a do-over. Sometimes, in life, you may even have an opportunity for a do-over, to correct your mistakes. But in the eternity to come there will be no do-overs. "Everyone has to die once, then face the consequences" (Hebrews 9:27 MSG). People who end up in hell will be consumed with never-ending, eternal regret.

Also, there will not be anyone in hell who will think they don't deserve to be there. Their memories will condemn them. I believe they will be able to remember every sin that they committed throughout their life.

If you've ever experienced excruciating pain, you might not have been able to think straight or coherently at that time. All you could think about was the awfulness of that pain. You may think that those suffering in hell won't be able to remember the past because of all the pain and suffering they will be enduring. Let's return to the story Jesus told of the rich man and Lazarus in Luke 16:19-31. The rich man had a conversation with Abraham. He was in agony, but he didn't have any problem remembering Lazarus's name and he also remembered that he had five brothers.

WHAT'S AT STAKE? (PART 3) – HELL

One of the most treasured books in my library is a little book written by J.A. James, an early Puritan writer, titled *The Anxious Inquirer*. I include this passage for your consideration.

> "You are an immortal creature, a being born for eternity, a creature that will never go out of existence. Millions of ages, as numerous as the sands upon the shore, and the drops of the ocean, and the leaves of all the forests on the globe, will not shorten the duration of your being; eternity, vast eternity, incomprehensible eternity, is before you. Every day brings you nearer to everlasting torments or felicity. You may die any moment; and you are as near to heaven or hell as you are to death. . . . How true, as well as solemn, are the words of Christ, 'What shall it profit a man, if he gain the whole world and lose his own soul; or what shall a man give in exchange for his soul?'
>
> "All the tears that ever have been or ever will be shed on the face of the earth, all the groans that ever have been or ever will be uttered, all the anguish that has been or ever will be endured by all the inhabitants of the world, through all the ages of time, do not make up an equal amount of misery to that which is included in the loss of one human soul. Justly therefore do you say, who are exposed to this misery, "What shall I do to be saved?"[45]

THE PENALTY FITS THE CRIME

Jesus was rejected, ridiculed, mocked, scorned, hated, despised, and eventually crucified; even though he had never done anything wrong or deserving of death. "But Jesus said, 'Father, forgive them; for they do not know what they are doing'" (Luke 23:34 NASB). We were enemies of God and yet "we were reconciled to God through the death of His Son . . ." (Romans 5:10 NASB).

An eternal God who had never known or experienced anything other than perfect love, perfect holiness, perfect peace, perfect beauty, perfect acceptance, agreed to suffer the most horrible death spawned in the mind of Satan. However, there are those who reject Him; they are the ones who dare ask the question, "How can a loving God prepare a hell as horrible as described in the Bible, and send people there?" There are several answers to that question beside the obvious one plainly seen here.

It was never God's intention for people to go to hell, and, even now, it still isn't. Hell was prepared for the devil and his angels. "The Lord does not delay and is not tardy or slow about what He promises, according to some people's conception of slowness, but He is long-suffering (extraordinarily patient) toward you, not desiring that any should perish, but that all should turn to repentance" (2 Peter 3:9).

In the spiritual realm, there are only two kingdoms. The kingdom of Satan (darkness) and the Kingdom of God (light). You either submit to God's authority and are made righteous in Him or you submit to Satan and become a slave to sin. God, your Creator, has given you the privilege to choose which one you want to serve. God never sends anyone to hell. Mankind chooses where they spend eternity. When they choose the kingdom of darkness, that's where they will spend eternity.

To question God's love is to believe the lie that God doesn't love us, and we know the father of lies is Satan. The question of God's

WHAT'S AT STAKE? (PART 3) – HELL

love is wrong because of where it originates. "Whenever he tells a lie, he speaks from his own nature, because he is a liar and the father of lies" (John 8:44 NASB). It's not a question of God's love—it's a question of man's love. The Bible removes all doubt about God's love in John 3:16.

After all, the penalty should fit the crime. This is certainly not an original argument on my part, yet I would be remiss if I were to leave it out. We are all familiar with the fact that some crimes receive a lesser sentence than others. The severity of the sentence depends on what was done, and on whom it was committed against. The common example given is the comparison of the same type of crime done against an ordinary citizen and one committed against a national or world leader. The one against an ordinary citizen might result in a sentence of a certain number of years, whereas one done against a national or world leader could result in a life sentence. This is because the impact of the same crime would be greater. Our sin and rejection of a perfectly holy, infinite, loving Creator requires an infinite sentence.

As mentioned earlier, the fires of hell will not cleanse nor remove the sins of those who commit them. No amount of suffering will suffice when atoning for sin. Only the shed blood of Jesus can remove sin. I will again refer to the story Jesus told of the rich man and Lazarus. When the rich man saw Lazurus with Abraham, his perspective of him had not changed with his circumstances.

He still viewed Lazurus as someone who could serve him. His god was still self. Whatever your sins were on earth will be the ones you carry into eternity. Because God hates sin, His wrath is eternal against the sin that will abide in you forever.

TAKING SIN TOO LIGHTLY

The problem is we take sin too lightly and it's because we've bought into more lies of Satan. They are as follows, "That's just a little lie." "You have every right to hate them or retaliate for what they did to you." "They wouldn't listen to you, so they don't deserve your help." "They made their bed, now they can lie in it." "You don't need to report that income on your tax statement. Just look at the way the government wastes our tax money." Or "Your employer doesn't pay you enough; you deserve more. They make millions—they won't miss that. It's not that big a deal."

To a holy God, that little sin is a big deal. "Your eyes are too pure to look at evil, and You cannot look at harm favorably" (Habakkuk 1:13 NASB). Will God wink at sin? Not on your life. The only ones who will be able to spend eternity in heaven will be those who are made perfect in Christ.

Satan loves it when people have no fear of hell. If what I'm describing could strike fear in the heart of only one person reading this, even to the point where they would get down on their knees and truly repent of their sin and accept Jesus as their Lord and Savior, then my efforts will have not be in vain.

FEAR AS A MOTIVATOR

There will be many who will protest that we shouldn't use fear to try to bring people to the Lord. Obviously, I disagree. Not all fear is bad. I doubt there's ever been a person who has raised a child that has not used fear at times to keep their children from harm; "Don't touch that hot stove—you'll get burned;" "Don't stick those scissors in

WHAT'S AT STAKE? (PART 3) – HELL

that electrical outlet—you'll get shocked;" "Don't do that—you'll get a spanking." Fear can be a great motivator.

The person who sincerely accepts Christ because of fear, and makes Him Lord of their life, will still experience the same indescribable love of Jesus, along with many other benefits—freedom, joy, peace, contentment, fulfillment, and purpose in life. This will be something that they've never known before. Best of all, they will spend eternity in heaven. There are times when the end justifies the means. "So if the Son sets you free, you really will be free" (John 8:36 NASB). Fear might motivate them to surrender to His Lordship, but once they begin to experience what true life is in Christ, their fear of Him will be overwhelmed by their love for Him.

Dear reader, if your heart is not right with God, I plead for you to not read another word until you repent and ask God to forgive you so that you might have eternal life and live with Him forever in heaven.

I pray that what follows will challenge all who read this to seriously consider where they are in their relationship with Christ. "Therefore, brothers and sisters, be all the more diligent to make certain about His calling and choice of you; for as long as you practice these things, you will never stumble" (2 Peter 1:10 NASB).

CHAPTER 12

REPENTANCE

> *"The church's problem today is in the misconception that we can add Christ to our lives, but not subtract sin. It is a change in belief without a change in behavior. It is revival without reformation, and without repentance."*
>
> —PATRICK MORLEY

When was the last time you heard your pastor, or any pastor, preach a message on repentance? How many times would you say your pastor has preached on repentance in the past year? Let's narrow it down even further. If your church still has an altar call, is there any mention made of the need to repent? I would venture to guess that the verses most quoted in an altar call are Romans 3:23 NASB: "for all have sinned and fall short of the glory of God;" Romans 3:10 NASB: "There is no righteous person, not even one;" and Romans 10:9-10 NASB:

"that if you confess with your mouth Jesus as Lord, and believe in your heart that God raised Him from the dead, you will be saved; for with the heart a person believes, resulting in righteousness, and with the mouth he confesses, resulting in salvation."

I think you will find it rare to hear the word repent now-a-days. Why do you think that is? Could it be that the word repent is considered too harsh in our culture or too confrontational? If you have to repent, then you are held accountable for your sin.

Very few in today's society want to accept responsibility for their actions. Many, in fact, are ready to say that they made mistakes, but few are ready to say that they sinned willfully. It's much easier to accept that "all have sinned" rather than say "I have sinned." In the Message translation Isaiah says: "Doom to you who use lies to sell evil, who haul sin to market by the truckload" (Isaiah 5:18). Many are sorry that they have sinned, but they are not ready to turn from their sin. When they do turn away from their sin, that's what true repentance is.

How well do you think it would go for a pastor of a church in America to say what John the Baptist did when he saw the Pharisees and the Sadducees coming to be baptized? "You offspring of vipers, who warned you to flee from the wrath to come? Therefore, produce fruit consistent with repentance; and do not assume that you can say to yourselves, 'We have Abraham as our father;' for I tell you that God is able, from these stones, to raise up children for Abraham" (Matthew 3:7-9 NASB). I love how my former pastor, John Lindell, in talking about fruit said, "Without the root (of repentance) there is not the fruit of repentance."

When we are introduced to John the Baptist in Matthew, his first recorded words were: "Repent, for the kingdom of heaven is at hand"

REPENTANCE

(Matthew 3:2 NASB). The subject matter of Jesus's first message was, "Repent, for the kingdom of heaven is at hand" (Matthew 4:17 NASB). On the day of Pentecost in Acts 2, Peter preached his first sermon after the outpouring of the Holy Spirit. "Now, when they heard this, they were pierced to the heart, and said to Peter and the rest of the apostles, 'Brothers, what are we to do?' Peter said to them, 'Repent, and each of you be baptized in the name of Jesus Christ for the forgiveness of your sins'" (Acts 37-38, NASB).

Fifty-one years later the Apostle Paul preached a message in the meeting at the Areopagus in Athens and said, "God is now proclaiming to mankind that all people everywhere are to repent ..." (Acts 17:30 NASB). He also preached, "But constantly and earnestly I bore testimony both to Jews and Greeks, urging them to turn in repentance [that is due] to God and to have faith in our Lord Jesus Christ [that is due Him]" (Acts 20:21).

Jesus called five of the seven churches in Revelation, Chapters 2-3, to repent. What happens when people refuse to repent? The writer to the Hebrews tells us what happens: "But instead warn (admonish, urge, and encourage) one another every day, as long as it is called Today, that none of you may be hardened [into settled rebellion] by the deceitfulness of sin [by the fraudulence, the stratagem, the trickery which the delusive glamor of his sin may play on him].... For who were they who heard and yet were rebellious and provoked [Him]? Was it not all those who came out of Egypt led by Moses? ... And to whom did He swear that they should not enter His rest, but to those who disobeyed [who had not listened to His word and who refused to be compliant or be persuaded]?" (Hebrews 3:13,16,18).

Now, what happens is that a person's heart is continually hardened every time the Holy Spirit brings conviction of sin, when they don't repent. There eventually comes a point where their heart becomes so hardened that they cannot repent.

We see this happening after Jesus calls the churches to repent in Revelation, Chapters 2-3. In Chapter 9, when the sixth angel blew his trumpet, a third of mankind was killed. It says in verse 20-21: "And the rest of humanity who were not killed by these plagues even then did not repent of [the worship of] the works of their [own] hands, so as to cease paying homage to the demons and idols of gold and silver and bronze and stone and wood, which can neither see nor hear nor move. And they did not repent of their murders or their practice of magic (sorceries) or their sexual vice or their thefts" (Revelation 9:20-21).

When 9/11 happened in America, there was a sudden jump in church attendance. On that day, 2,997 people were killed.

The current world population is somewhere just over 8 billion people. In Chapters 6 and 9 of Revelation, a third and then a fourth of mankind are killed by the seal and trumpet judgments. This happens after the rapture.

Because we have no way of knowing how many will go in the rapture when Christ returns, let's use a conservative estimate of ten percent of the world's population, which would be 800 million. To make it easy, let's round that up to 1 billion even. That would mean that even when over 2.4 billion people die it doesn't seem to faze the survivors—they don't repent. That's a perfect picture of a hardened heart.

BOWLS OF WRATH

Revelation 16 introduces seven angels who pour out seven bowls of God's wrath and indignation on the earth. The first bowl afflicted

REPENTANCE

painful ulcers (sores) on those who received the mark of the beast and worshipped him. The second bowl resulted in the sea being turned to blood and every living thing in the sea perished. The result of the third bowl was the rivers and springs of water turned into blood.

When the fourth bowl was poured out, the sun was permitted to burn humanity with fierce heat and people were severely burned. So, what did they do? Surely they finally repented, right? "And they reviled and blasphemed the name of God, who has control of these plagues, and they did not repent of their sins [felt no regret, contrition, and compunction for their waywardness, refusing to amend their ways] to give Him glory."

Then there was the fifth bowl which was darkness on the throne of the beast, "and people gnawed their tongues for the torment [of their excruciating distress and severe pain] and blasphemed the God of heaven because of their anguish and their ulcers (sores), and they did not deplore their wicked deeds or repent [for what they had done]."

"The sixth angel poured out his bowl on the great river Euphrates, and its water was dried up to prepare the way for the kings from the East. Then I saw three impure spirits that looked like frogs; they came out of the mouth of the dragon, out of the mouth of the beast and out of the mouth of the false prophet. They are demonic spirits that perform signs, and they go out to the kings of the whole world, to gather them for the battle on the great day of God Almighty."

Finally, the seventh angel poured out his bowl and, among other things, it said: "And great (excessively oppressive) hailstones, as heavy as a talent [between fifty and sixty pounds], of immense size, fell from the sky on the people; and men blasphemed God for the plague of the hail, so very great was [the torture] of that plague" (Revelation 16:2-4,8-14,21).

There may be some, in reading these passages revealing the wrath of God being poured out upon all of mankind, who may miss an important truth. Some may see the God of all mercy as having exhausted His mercy so that all that remains is His wrath. That could never happen because God is infinite, thus His mercy is infinite. When God extends mercy to someone, His mercy is not diminished in the slightest.

You see, the phrase repeated in the above passages is that "they did not repent." From this, the sense I get as these events unfold before the Apostle John's eyes is that of his incredulity because they didn't repent despite all that happened. In other words, John is saying: "Can you believe this? After all that's happened to them, they still don't repent?"

PAST HISTORY

I'm sure John was familiar with the writings of the prophet Habakkuk in the Old Testament. Habakkuk lived and prophesied in a time when Judah, Israel's southern kingdom, was ripe for judgment. His words in Chapter 1 still echo down the corridors of time to current day America. "God, how long do I have to cry out for help before you listen? How many times do I have to yell, 'Help! Murder! Police!' before you come to the rescue? Why do you force me to look at evil, stare trouble in the face day after day? Anarchy and violence break out, quarrels and fights all over the place. Law and order fall to pieces. Justice is a joke. The wicked have the righteous hamstrung and stand justice on its head" (Habakkuk 1:2-4 MSG).

The current refrain from politicians and the news media today is that "Nobody is above the law." And yet I am convinced that there are millions of people, not only in America, but worldwide, who would

REPENTANCE

say that statement couldn't be further from the truth. If ever there were a time in history when the world was ripe for judgment, it is now.

Revelation 3:19 (NASB) says: "Those whom I love, I rebuke and discipline; therefore be zealous and repent."

"In the midst of mounting world misery and mystery there 'runs one golden thread of purpose, not the iron thread of doom.' God has gracious ends in view. There are things worse than trouble, worse than pain, worse than death. Sin, to God, is the only unendurable, more intolerable even than hell. Yes, God hates hell, hates it more than we do, but He hates sin more than He hates hell. If the world's mounting misery will crowd men to Christ and make hell the emptier, they are better than sin. Such is the wisdom of God in a mystery."[46]

All of us at some point in our lives could identify with how Habakkuk felt. Have you ever felt like your prayers go no higher than the ceiling? Like the heavens are brass? Like God has become deaf to your cries? What follows in the rest of Chapters 1 and 2 is God's response to the prophet's pleas. The Lord informs him that He is going to send the Babylonian army to get the kingdom of Judah's attention, a nation renowned for their cruelty, to try and bring them to repentance.

Since Judah had become so hardened in their sin, God, due to His great love for them, had to use severe measures to bring them to repentance.

"Distress that drives us to God does that. It turns us around. It gets us back in the way of salvation. We never regret that kind of pain. But those who let distress drive them away from God are full of regrets, end up on a deathbed of regrets" (2 Corinthians 7:10 MSG).

I love Habakkuk's response, in Chapter 3:1, to what the Lord declared He was going to do. He bursts forth in rapturous singing. "A prayer of Habakkuk the prophet, set to wild, enthusiastic, and triumphal music." To be honest, the prophet's response to the judgment God is going to bring upon His people seems out of place. This is because the horizon is filled with the dark clouds of impending doom that is going to come upon the nation he loves; despite this, he is dancing with joy. How can this be? Well, that is because of what he writes in verse 2: "O Lord, I have heard the report of You and was afraid. O Lord, revive Your work in the midst of the years, in the midst of the years make [Yourself] known! In wrath [earnestly] remember love, pity, and mercy."

He's celebrating because he sees revival coming. A revival of holiness and repentance. He was celebrating because he knew that even in God's wrath His motives are love, pity, and mercy. We saw something similar happen in America on September 11, 2001. After 9/11 there was a boom in church attendance. Sadly, it faded as quickly as it came.

Now, let us return to Revelation. This is where the 7 years of tribulation to come is recorded; some of the events I have mentioned above. The events that occur in the first three-and-a-half years of the tribulation begin in Chapter 6 and continue through Chapter 12. As horrible as the wars, famines, pestilence, earthquakes, and signs in the heavens, and on the earth are in the first three-and-a-half years, they pale in comparison to what happens at the beginning of Chapter 13. What follows in these last three-and-a-half years is known as the Great Tribulation.

In the past, when reading about the wrath of God in these chapters, I viewed His wrath as punitive. All I could see were "sinners

REPENTANCE

in the hands of an angry God." I pictured Him saying something like your parents may have said to you, "I've had it up to here." That's not something I ever wanted to hear growing up. It was like the "straw that broke the camel's back." They were done, and they weren't going to accept any more of what we were doing.

Another example that made me think about this passage is found in Revelation 9:4-6 when the locusts are released from the Abyss (the bottomless pit). They are instructed to "only [to attack] such human beings as do not have the seal (mark) of God on their foreheads. They were not permitted to kill them, but to torment (distress, vex) them for five months; and the pain caused them was like the torture of a scorpion when it stings a person. And in those days people will seek death and will not find it; and they will yearn to die, but death evades and flees from them."

All that some can see here is a vindictive, sadistic, angry God who makes them suffer so terribly that they wish for death and even seek it but can't find it. What we can miss in these verses are the words "They were not permitted to kill them" (verse 5). He did not allow them to kill them because His ultimate goal is to bring them to repentance, it's not just to inflict pain and suffering.

What changed my perception of the wrath of God was reading how often John mentioned that they refused to repent. I believe John couldn't believe what he was seeing. What I've come to realize is that every time they refused to repent, their hearts were becoming harder and more obstinate in their sin. Thus, the wrath of God increased as He tried to bring them to repentance. The greater the wrath of God, the greater His love and mercy is revealed for mankind.

You may have heard your parents say this when disciplining you, "This is going to hurt me more than it's going to hurt you." As a child, hearing that said made you think they were crazy for saying that. But when you become a parent, you understand. You learn that when discipline is done right it's not being done out of anger, but out of love for your children; it's done with the desire to stop them from continuing down the wrong path. After all, the last thing you ever want to do is hurt them.

The most extreme love ever witnessed by mankind was when God the Father gave His only begotten Son to take our place; when Jesus Christ, the Son of God, took God's righteous judgment of our sin upon Himself, He suffered the cruelest of deaths for us that we might have life, and that more abundantly.

The truth is, God's wrath is not against man, but against the sin in man. The only way that sin can be removed from man is through Jesus Christ. When man refuses to let go of his sin, and refuses to repent, then the final judgment of sin is the fires of hell. This means that, since the retainer of sin is man, the retainer of sin suffers the judgment sin brings for all eternity.

"Say to them, as I live, says the Lord God, I have no pleasure in the death of the wicked, but rather that the wicked turn from his way and live. Turn back, turn back from your evil ways, for why will you die" (Ezekiel 33:1).

CHAPTER 13

ARE YOU READY TO MAKE A DECISION?

*"I am not a product of my circumstances.
I am a product of my decisions."*

—STEPHEN COVEY

From Krista Tippet's book, *Becoming Wise: An Inquiry into the Mystery and Art of Living*, it says, "We have grown up in a world where there were answers for everything. And the answers felt too small. But I also find a question to be a mighty form of words, and I have learned a few things about questions. I have learned that questions elicit answers in their likeness—that answers rise or fall to the questions they meet. We've all seen this. We've all experienced it. It's very hard to respond to a combative question with anything but a combative answer. It's almost impossible to transcend a simplistic question with anything but a simplistic answer. But the opposite is also true: it's hard to resist a generous question. This is a skill that needs relearning, but we all have it in us to ask questions that invite, that draw forth searching in dignity and revelation. There is something redemptive and lifegiving about asking a better question.

"And it is a deep truth in science, and also in each of our lives, that we are shaped as much by the quality of the questions we're asking at any given point as by the answers we have it in us to give. Those moments in our lives when a better quality of question rises up in us, stops us in our tracks—those are pivot points."[47]

The title of this chapter is a simple question but it is one that can have eternal consequences. It is my hope that this will be a pivotal point in the life of those reading this. If, in reading this book, the Holy Spirit is convicting you about the way you are living out your faith; what are you going to do? Is it that you have never accepted Jesus Christ as your LORD and SAVIOR? What are you going to do about that? Do you need to repent? If so, are you going to put it off and be an honorary member of the Procrastinators Club of America?

When we speak of God, the word we use to describe Him is infinite. In other words, He's without limits. He is outside of time and space (omnipresent); He's infinite in power (omnipotence); and He's infinite in knowledge (omniscience).

Here's a question that may seem to have an obvious answer in regard to the last paragraph. Can we as puny human beings limit a God who is limitless? Our natural response would be "NO, NO WAY!" However, that's not the case. This may blow your mind, but the Bible says we can. "Time and again they pushed him to the limit, provoked Israel's Holy God" (Psalm 78:41 MSG).

This Psalm is about the Israelites being delivered out of Egypt and wandering in the wilderness for forty years. It was written by Asaph, one of the worship leaders appointed by King David. Time and time again God wanted to bless the Israelites but they limited his blessings because of their unbelief.

John the Baptist, when speaking of Jesus in John 3:34, said this, "For since He Whom God has sent speaks the words of God [proclaims God's own message], God does not give Him His Spirit sparingly or by measure, but boundless is the gift God makes of His Spirit!" Another word for boundless is limitlessness.

And yet we read in Matthew 13:58 (NASB), "And He did not do many miracles there because of their unbelief." Throughout the Gospels we are told that all who were brought to Jesus that were blind, sick, lame, or demon possessed, were healed.

His power was not limited when He came to His hometown of Nazareth. He could have done the same things in Nazareth that He did everywhere else. But because the people saw Him only as a local hometown boy, those who were sick limited Him by not coming to Him or by bringing only a few of those in need of miracles to Him.

RETURNING TO SIN

In Genesis, one of the most significant events in the history of Israel as a nation began in Egypt. God sent Moses to deliver them out of their bondage to the Egyptians. This became a symbol of our deliverance from sin and death through faith in Jesus Christ.

The record in the Old Testament of Israel is like a looping video that repeats itself over and over again. God delivers them and they serve him for a while. But then they turn away from Him to worship false gods. God judges them by allowing their enemies to bring them into bondage again. Eventually their suffering causes them to repent and call on God to save them. Since God is a God of great mercy, love, and compassion, He sends them a deliverer.

This is where the image of a looping video begins. Just repeat the paragraph above verbatim. Then do it again. And again. And again.

You get the picture.

God the Father, sent Jesus to Earth to deliver us from the bondage of sin. But many Christians are like the ancient Israelites. They receive Jesus as their Savior but after a while they return to their old ways. This same Jesus is coming back soon for His Bride, which is the Church. In speaking of His return in Luke 18:8, Jesus asks the question, "However, when the Son of Man comes, will He find persistence in] faith on the earth?"

CHAPTER 14

ETERNAL SECURITY?

"We... ought ourselves to fear, lest by chance, after the knowledge of Christ, if we do things displeasing to God, we obtain no further forgiveness of sins, but be shut out from his kingdom."

—IRENAEUS (*AGAINST HERESIES* IV:27:2)

In the next chapter, we will take a look at the Parable of the Ten Virgins, which is found in Matthew 25:1-13. There is one important part of this parable that we need to consider first. It's the part about the five wise and the five foolish virgins. I hesitated to mention this, because it brings up a very controversial subject, but I feel it needs to be addressed. It is between the Calvinist and the Armenians. The controversy is whether a born-again believer can lose their salvation.

The quote by Irenaeus is an example of many of the early church fathers who taught against eternal security. "Before the Reformation, belief in forms of eternal security were anecdotal. Besides, in the early 5th century, the Augustinian soteriology view of predestination by predetermination emerged, though it did not endorse eternal security."[48]

There were two different movements which arose around the 16th and 17th centuries, between theologian John Calvin and his followers, and Jacob Arminus, and his followers. There are two passages of Scripture that are the most often quoted scriptures in this controversy to buttress their arguments for their beliefs. John 10:26-30 NASB (Calvinist), "But you do not believe, because you are not of My sheep. My sheep listen to My voice, and I know them, and they follow Me; and I give them eternal life, and they will never perish; and no one will snatch them out of My hand. My Father, who has given them to Me, is greater than all; and no one is able to snatch them out of the Father's hand. I and the Father are one."

The second scripture is Hebrews 6:4-6 (Arminian), "For it is impossible, in the case of those who have once been enlightened and have tasted of the heavenly gift and have been made partakers of the Holy Spirit, and have tasted the good word of God and the powers of the age to come, and then have fallen away, to restore them again to repentance, since they again crucify to themselves the Son of God and put Him to open shame."

In the footnotes of the NASB translation, in regard to the phrase "then have fallen away" says, "Or committed apostasy; i.e., renounced the faith."

There are five main doctrines ascribed to by the Calvinist, but the one I feel compelled to address is the one most commonly referred to

ETERNAL SECURITY?

as eternal security; or once saved, always saved. It is not my desire to do a deep dive into this theological debate, but rather to simply state the differences, as I understand them.

This Calvinist tenet of faith, also known as the perseverance of the saints, is that once you are saved, you become "heirs of God and joint heirs with Jesus Christ (Romans 8:17);" you become part of the family of God. Once this happens nothing, and no one, can remove you from the family of God, ever. I am one of those who are convinced that this belief in eternal security has resulted in many believers living no different from the world, because they can't lose their salvation.

The problem arises when someone who has made a confession of faith in Christ, who bears the fruit of a changed life, but sometime in the future, sometimes many years later, returns to a life of sin, and dies without ever repenting. Calvinist use this parable of the five wise, and the five foolish virgins, to assert that the five foolish virgins are those who claim to be Christians, but were never actually saved. And that could very well be the case. Only God knows for sure.

Based on my study, the Bible clearly says that we can lose our salvation, which would land me in the Arminian camp, who believe that a true born-again believer can lose their salvation.

If you are a strong Calvinist, or lean that way, please hear me out. I struggled greatly whether to include this subject matter. I felt compelled to for this one simple reason—my passion has been ignited by what I perceive to be a lack of holiness within the Church. I believe the doctrine of eternal security can, and does more often than not, lead to the abuse of God's standards of holiness.

I would like to compare this controversy to Pascal's wager which was a "practical argument for belief in God formulated by French mathematician and philosopher Blaise Pascal. In his Pensées (1657-58), Pascal applied elements of game theory to show that belief in Christian religion is rational. He argued that people can choose to believe in God or can choose to not believe in God, and that God either exists or he does not. Under these conditions, if a person believes in the Christian God and this God actually exists, they gain infinite happiness; if a person does not believe in the Christian God and God exists, they receive infinite suffering.

"On the other hand, if a person believes in the Christian God and God does not exist, then they receive some finite disadvantages from a life of Christian living; and if a person does not believe in this God and God does not exist, then they receive some finite pleasure from a life lived unhindered by Christian morality."[49]

If it's true born-again believers can lose their salvation, and it could affect change in those reading this, who have no concern of how they live in this present world because they cannot lose their salvation in the world to come, then by necessity, I must warn them. If I'm wrong, it doesn't change anything in their future. What follows are a few examples of why I believe the way I do.

Typology is prevalent in Scripture, a type being a symbol representing something else. All throughout Scripture, oil is a type or symbol of the Holy Spirit. The five wise took oil in their jars along with their lamps. It says that the five foolish virgins were unprepared for the bridegroom's arrival because they did not take any oil with them. "And the foolish said to the wise, 'Give us some of your oil, for our lamps are going out'" (Matthew 25:8). Their lamps were once filled with oil (Holy Spirit) but now they were running out. This would indicate to me that the five foolish virgins were a symbol of those believers who were once filled with the Holy Spirit, born of the Spirit, true born-again believers, who have lost what they once had.

This is a very sobering thought in the sense that some Bible scholars believe that the five foolish virgins, half of the ten, represent fifty percent of the church who claim to be born again, who will be left behind at the rapture of the church.

WE ARE HIS BRIDE

Again, throughout the Old Testament, God refers to his chosen people, Israel, as his bride. "For your Maker is your Husband—the Lord of hosts is His name—and the Holy One of Israel is your Redeemer; the God of the whole earth He is called" (Isaiah 54:5).

In the New Testament, the Church is referred to as the Bride of Christ. "For I am jealous for you with a godly jealousy; for I betrothed you to one husband, to present you *as* a pure virgin to Christ. But I am afraid that, as the serpent deceived Eve by his trickery, your minds will be led astray from sincere and pure devotion to Christ. For if one comes and preaches another Jesus whom we have not preached, or you receive a different spirit which you have not received, or a different gospel which you have not accepted, this you tolerate very well!" (2 Corinthians 11:2-4 NASB).

Paul was afraid that the Corinthians would abandon their faith and be deceived by Satan, even as Eve was. When Eve was deceived what happened? It ended in spiritual death for her and for Adam, who joined her in eating the forbidden fruit from the tree of the knowledge of good and evil.

Paul said that the Corinthians were like a pure virgin. Could that be interpreted any other way than Paul was saying they were born again by the Spirit of God? If those in Corinth were deceived like Eve, and accepted a different spirit and a different gospel than what Paul preached to them, if they did not repent, they would have lost their purity and would no longer be acceptable to Christ as his bride. Christ is coming for a pure, unblemished, and holy bride.

WHAT ABOUT DIVORCE?

God, speaking through the prophet Malachi said that he hates divorce (Malachi 2:16). Jesus affirmed this when he said, "But from the beginning of creation, God created them male and female. For this reason, a man shall leave his father and mother, and the two shall become one flesh; so, they are no longer two, but one flesh. Therefore, what God has joined together, no person is to separate" (Mark 10:6-9 NASB).

The marriage between a man and woman, where they become one, is likened to Christ and the Church becoming one flesh. And yet in a marriage Jesus said there are grounds for divorce, but only for two reasons. One is in the case of infidelity. The other is given by Paul in 1 Corinthians 7:12-16, in which a divorce is allowed when an unbeliever wants to divorce a Christian. In both instances when the marriage bond is broken, their marriage and their relationship are dead.

Because God hates divorce, I believe in both instances mentioned above, divorce should be the last resort. There have been many marriages that have been restored through forgiveness, reconciliation, and a long process of restoration and the rebuilding of trust. In the case of an unbelieving spouse who refuses to remain married, you may be left with no choice, even though you love them.

Because a marriage between a man and woman is a type, symbol, or shadow of the believer's relationship to God, then how is it that it's impossible to lose our salvation? Is it right for us as God's children to have grounds for divorce, but God doesn't?

This is what God told the Israelites: "And I saw, even though [Judah knew] that for this very cause of committing adultery (idolatry) I [the Lord] had put faithless Israel away and given her a bill of divorce; yet her faithless and treacherous sister Judah was not afraid, but she also went and played the harlot [following after idols]" (Jeremiah 3:8).

The Israelites were His chosen inheritance and because of their worship of the idols of other nations, which He called spiritual adultery, He divorced them. It wasn't after the first time they committed spiritual adultery, but only after they persisted in their sin and rebellion against His laws. He first exhausted every means possible to get them to repent and return to Him before He divorced them. Later, in verse 12, He tells the Israelites through Jeremiah that He would receive them back only if they acknowledged their iniquity and their guilt. In other words, only if they would repent. Only a remnant returned, and God restored them because He will keep His promises to His people. But His marriage to the rest who refused was ended. That marriage relationship was dead.

History is replete with stories of pastors and laity alike who were on fire for God. They lived lives of holiness and led many to Christ, but somewhere along the way they backslid and returned to the muck and mire of sin. God in his great mercy will receive them back, but only if they truly repent.

THE GREAT APOSTASY

Paul, in 2 Thessalonians 2:3, says, "Let no one in any way deceive or entrap you, for that day will not come unless the apostasy comes first [that is, the great rebellion, the abandonment of the faith by professed Christians]."

Paul was correcting their misconception that the day of the Lord had already come. According to Strong's Concordance, the Greek word translated here as apostasy means "defection from truth—falling away, forsake."[50]

Paul was speaking of believers, who in the last days before the coming of Christ, once believed the truth of the Gospel of Jesus Christ, but will defect from the truth and forsake it completely, never to return.

As said previously, many claim what Jesus said in John 10:28-29 (NASB), proves that once we are saved, we can never lose our salvation. "and I give them eternal life, and they will never perish; and no one will snatch them out of My hand. My Father, who has given them to Me, is greater than all; and no one is able to snatch them out of the Father's hand."

I'm in total agreement that no power in heaven, on earth, or in hell, can ever remove a believer who is wholly committed to God, from His hand. But those believers who defect from the truth, totally forsaking it, can remove themselves from His hand. And even then, God, because He loves them so much, will do everything in His power, all the way up to the point, yet short of, forcing them to remain in him. God has given us free will and He will not force someone to go to heaven.

ABIDING IN HIM

Just one more example of why I believe we can lose our salvation. "I am the True Vine, and My Father is the Vinedresser. Any branch in Me that does not bear fruit [that stops bearing] He cuts away (trims off, takes away) . . . Dwell in Me, and I will dwell in you. [Live in Me, and I will live in you.] Just as no branch can bear fruit of itself without abiding in (being vitally united to) the vine, neither can you bear fruit unless you abide in Me. I am the Vine; you are the branches. Whoever lives in Me and I in him bears much (abundant) fruit. However, apart from Me [cut off from vital union with Me] you can do nothing. If a person does not dwell in Me, he is thrown out like a [broken-off] branch, and withers; such branches are gathered up and thrown into the fire, and they are burned" (John 15:1-2,4-6).

The only way we can be in Christ is if we are born again. Jesus says He is the vine, and we are the branches. If we are not fruitful, God the Father, will remove us from the vine. What is the fruit that God the Father requires of us? Paul tells us in Philippians 1:9-11 (NLT), "I pray that your love will overflow more and more, and that you will keep on growing in knowledge and understanding. For I want you to understand what really matters, so that you may live pure and blameless lives until the day of Christ's return. May you always be filled with the fruit of your salvation—the righteous character produced in your life by Jesus Christ—for this will bring much glory and praise to God."

The fruit the Father requires of us is the righteousness of Christ. The Father will not allow us to drag the name of Christ through the mud. He will remove any who do not continue to "live pure and blameless lives until the day of Christ's return." "Until" implies that we could stop short of living "pure and blameless lives."

"For it is time for judgment to begin with the household of God; and if it begins with us first, what will be the outcome for those who do not obey the gospel of God?" (1 Peter 4:17 NASB).

Have you noticed the headlines in the news lately (2024)? There have been several prominent pastors who have either stepped down, or have been removed from their churches because of moral failures or other sins that have become known. I believe Jesus is getting His church ready for His return. The Lord is beginning to clean house, starting with the leaders. But make no mistake, He will not stop there. Sadly, I believe there will be many more occurrences of this nature, not just those pastors in the limelight. Mark my words, it will not be just pastors. It will be the laity as well. He is not doing this to bring shame, but repentance.

We have all failed from time to time. I will be quick to admit my failures, but when I do I repent and ask God to forgive me, He is true to his Word, He will forgive me. "If we [freely] admit that we have sinned and confess our sins, He is faithful and just [true to His own nature and promises] and will forgive our sins and cleanse us continually from all unrighteousness [our wrongdoing, everything not in conformity with His will and purpose]" (1 John 1:9).

ETERNAL SECURITY?

ARE YOU TOO GREAT A SINNER?

God wants to do a miraculous transformation of our lives and conform us into His image. It doesn't matter how much you have done. Some think they are too great a sinner. They think they've gone too far. Imagine with me, if you will, all the people that God has forgiven, from the time of Adam and Eve to this present day. Think of all the sins they committed. He forgave them all. Take all their sins together and compare your sins to theirs. You may be the worst sinner that's ever walked the face of the earth, but it won't equal the amount of all their sins. So, yours aren't too much for Him to forgive. "The Lord is close to those who are of a broken heart and saves such as are crushed with sorrow for sin and are humbly and thoroughly penitent" (Psalm 34:18).

"For you were called to freedom, brothers and sisters; only do not turn your freedom into an opportunity for the flesh but serve one another through love.... But I say, walk by the Spirit, and you will not carry out the desire of the flesh. For the desire of the flesh is against the Spirit, and the Spirit against the flesh; for these are in opposition to one another, in order to keep you from doing whatever you want... Now the deeds of the flesh are evident, which are: sexual immorality, impurity, indecent behavior, idolatry, witchcraft, hostilities, strife, jealousy, outbursts of anger, selfish ambition, dissensions, factions, envy, drunkenness, carousing, and things like these, of which I forewarn you, just as I have forewarned you, that those who practice such things will not inherit the Kingdom of God" (Galatians 5:13,16-17,19-21 NASB).

I am well aware that there will be many much more learned than I who will disagree with what they've just read. Knowing this, I would like to make a final plea.

BOUNDARIES

As I'm writing this, a piece of conceptual art titled "Comedian," a banana duct taped to a white wall, just sold at Sotheby's. After reading several articles about this "work of art," the conclusion is that the definition of art has no boundaries. Some even suggested that the artist, Maurizio Cattelan, created his work to demonstrate the absurdity of no boundaries.

They evidently should have put up barriers around the exhibit because a person walked up to it, removed the banana, and promptly took a bite of it. He was a "performance artist," acting out his supposed artistic expression.

Five years before this most recent sale, three other editions sold for between $120,000 and $150,000. You would think even one person buying this self-styled art for that amount of money would be crazy. But there were two more as well. But it gets even crazier. It just sold again for $6.2 million. The purchaser said that in a few days, after receiving it, he would honor this unique artistic expression by eating it.

There may not be any boundaries in the art world, but there are still standards in God's kingdom. In the last couple of years I have noticed more and more believers living together outside of marriage, who attend church as if there's nothing wrong with their lifestyle. I emphasize lifestyle because it's not just a failure or sin committed in a moment of weakness. Others wouldn't dare do this openly, but often sleep with their significant others in secret.

I have also noticed a coarsening of language and lifestyle in people of faith. Cursing, lying, lust, greed, unforgiveness, hatred, revenge, and much, much more, are justified on the grounds that everyone else does it because society is okay with it.

It might be OK with society, but let me say without equivocation, God will not overlook it! Many have bought into that lie by that great deceiver, Satan. If this is your lifestyle, then you are not saved: you must repent or you will be lost for all eternity.

"No one who abides in Him [who lives and remains in communion with and in obedience to Him—deliberately, knowingly, and habitually] commits (practices) sin. No one who [habitually] sins has either seen or known Him [recognized, perceived, or understood Him, or has had an experiential acquaintance with Him]" (1 John 3:6).

CHAPTER 15

IMPORTANCE OF PROPHECY

"For I am God, and there is no one else; I am God, and there is none like Me, declaring the end and the result from the beginning, and from ancient times the things that are not yet done."

—ISAIAH 46:9-10

There are many prophecies in the Bible that let us know the signs of the time when Jesus will return. The Pharisees and the Sadducees came to Jesus asking Him to show them a sign (miracle) that would attest to his divine authority. Jesus rebuked them by saying, "You know how to interpret the appearance of the sky, but you cannot interpret the signs of the times" (Luke 18:8).

Luke, Chapter 19, records the triumphal entry of Jesus into Jerusalem prior to his crucifixion. "As He was approaching [the city], at the descent of the Mount of Olives, the whole crowd of the disciples began to rejoice and to praise God [extolling Him exultantly and] loudly for all the mighty miracles and works of power that they had witnessed, crying, 'Blessed (celebrated with praises) is the King Who comes in the name of the Lord! Peace in heaven [freedom there from all the distresses that are experienced as the result of sin] and glory (majesty and splendor) in the highest [heaven]!'" (Luke 19:37-38).

The Pharisees were indignant when they heard this and told Jesus to rebuke them for what they were claiming. What follows now in verses 43-44, is Jesus's prophecy concerning the coming destruction of Jerusalem in 70 AD. Jesus said this would happen, "[all] because you did not come progressively to recognize and know and understand [from observation and experience] the time of your visitation [that is, when God was visiting you, the time in which God showed Himself gracious toward you and offered you salvation through Christ]" (Luke 19:44).

Many of the Pharisees and Sadducees could quote most, if not all, of the Old Testament but they didn't recognize the times, nor their Messiah standing right in front of them. There are many pastors, teachers, and ordinary believers, just like the Pharisees and Sadducees, who are clueless to the times we are living in.

As much as 27 percent of the Bible is about prophecy. There are many pastors who rarely teach on prophecy. As a result, they are ignoring one-third of the Bible. This will result in many present-day believers being like the five foolish virgins who were unprepared for the groom's appearance. Now, it would take too long to explain why pastor's avoid prophecy, but if you are one of those pastors, how will you answer those in your congregation who ask, "Why aren't you teaching us about prophecy?"

GALILEAN WEDDINGS

In Matthew 25, Jesus tells the parable of the ten virgins—five who were wise, and five who were foolish. All but one of the disciples, Judas, were from Galilee and would have at once recognized the marriage customs between a man and a woman that were married there.

Jesus used the imagery of a Galilean wedding as a foreshadowing for the rapture of the Church and the Marriage Supper of the Lamb. First there was the betrothal (engagement) of the bride and groom. It was at this time that a contract would be signed and the groom, or the parents of the groom, would pay a dowry to the bride, or to the parents of the bride. Gifts would then be exchanged, and the groom would offer the bride the "Cup of Joy" (wine) to drink from. She could either accept or reject it. If she accepted it the engagement would then be official.

The first phase of this ceremony occurs when we accept Jesus Christ as our Savior. The cost of the dowry for God the Father, was the precious life of His only begotten Son, Jesus Christ. The blood He shed upon the cross washed away all of our sin and made us acceptable to Him.

The groom would then say, "You are now consecrated to me by the laws of Moses and I will not drink from this cup again until I drink it with you in my father's house."[51]

At the last supper when Jesus shared the cup of wine with His disciples He said, " But I say to you, I will not drink of this fruit of the vine from now on until that day when I drink it with you, new, in My Father's kingdom" (Matthew 26:29 NASB).

The groom would then leave the bride and return to his father's house. In the coming months he will add a room to his father's house for the bride. I'm trying hard right now as I write this to keep from crying with joy as I anticipate what Jesus said to his disciples in John 14:2-3 (NASB): "In My Father's house are many rooms; if that were not so, I would have told you, because I am going there to prepare a place for you. And if I go and prepare a place for you, I am coming again and will take you to Myself, so that where I am, there you also will be."

We are now in the second phase, the betrothal period. After His resurrection Jesus returned to the Father to prepare a place for us. Most Bible scholars believe Jesus died in either 30 or 33 A.D. At the time I'm writing this, if he died in 30 A.D., that would be 1,994 years. If it was 33 A.D., then it would be 1,991 years. This is how long He has been preparing a room for us.

We've been told that heaven is a beautiful place. If Christ has been preparing a place for us for almost 2,000 years, then we know it's going to be beyond description. Paul says this when he writes to the Corinthians, "What eye has not seen and ear has not heard and has not entered into the heart of man, [all that] God has prepared (made and keeps ready) for those who love Him [who hold Him in affectionate reverence, promptly obeying Him and gratefully recognizing the benefits He has bestowed]" (1 Corinthians 2:9).

John, in Revelation 21:9, writes about one of the angels that carried John away to a high mountain and showed him the new Jerusalem, the city which Jesus has prepared for us. The angel measured the city which was laid out in a square, and it was 12,000 stadia (approximately 1,400-1,500 miles). It is in the shape of a cube because the height, width, and length are equal.

IMPORTANCE OF PROPHECY

"Given the dimensions of a 1,400-mile cube, if the city consisted of different levels (we don't know this), and if each story were a generous twelve feet high, the city could have over 600,000 stories. If they were on different levels, billions of people could occupy the New Jerusalem, with many square miles per person."[52] If that doesn't impress you, then nothing will. That's just its dimensions. To get the entire picture of this beautiful city, read verse 10 to the end of Chapter 21.

ONLY FATHER KNOWS

Here is the unique thing about weddings in Galilee, and it's something that would strike terror in the hearts of brides today. Neither the bride, groom, nor anyone else in the whole town knew when the wedding would take place, only the father of the groom knew because he was the one who made the decision when the couple would get married. The father of the groom would announce the day of the wedding, so the bride always had to be ready. As Gomer Pyle would say, "Surprise, surprise!"

Because living in Galilee in the time of Christ was not easy and was short on excitement, weddings were huge events that everyone looked forward to. The father of the groom would not announce the wedding day until the son had the room ready and all of the preparations were made. This process would usually take up to a year. I'm sure that during this time the bride would be keeping tabs on the progress the groom was making. Either by having her friends keeping her aware of the progress being made or possibly even the groom would let her know when the room addition was ready, and the preparations for the wedding supper were just about finished.

Can you imagine the excitement building in anticipation of the wedding? I can see the headlines in bold relief in the local newspaper, "JESSE, THE SON OF OBED HAS COMPLETED THE ROOM ADDITION! Better get ready! We're going to have a wedding!"

Now we can understand what Jesus meant, when speaking of returning for His Bride, He said, "But of that [exact] day and hour no one knows, not even the angels of heaven, nor the Son, but only the Father" (Matthew 24:36).

At the beginning of Matthew 24, the disciples had asked Jesus this question, "Tell us, when will this take place, and what will be the sign of Your coming and of the end (the completion, the consummation) of the age?" (Matthew 24:3). I love the fact that the AMPC adds clarity by using the word "consummation." That is a word that's associated with the wedding day.

What follows in the rest of the chapter is Jesus telling the disciples about signs to watch for that will indicate His soon return. He tells them, "So also when you see these signs, all taken together, coming to pass, you may know of a surety that He is near, at the very doors" (Matthew 24:33).

We are not ignorant of the fact that people have been led astray by false prophets that have claimed that they knew the exact day when the Lord was returning. In this same chapter, Matthew 24:42-43, Jesus made it clear again, "Therefore be on the alert, for you do not know which day your Lord is coming. But be sure of this, that if the head of the house had known at what time of the night the thief was coming, he would have been on the alert and would not have allowed his house to be broken into."

IMPORTANCE OF PROPHECY

The Apostle Paul, in writing to the church at Thessalonica, confirms what Jesus said about the signs indicating His soon return. "But you, brothers and sisters, are not in darkness, so that the day would overtake you like a thief. For you are all sons of light and sons of the day; we do not belong either to the night or to darkness. Accordingly, then, let us not sleep, as the rest do, but let us keep wide awake (alert, watchful, cautious, and on our guard) and let us be sober (calm, collected, and circumspect)" (1 Thessalonians 5:4-6, NASB).

The brothers and sisters that Paul was writing to were born again believers, children of God. "The Spirit Himself [thus] testifies together with our own spirit, [assuring us] that we are children of God" (Romans 8:16). As His Church, we are His Bride, and He will not leave us in the dark concerning the day of His return. We won't know the exact day, but everyone I know who has studied the signs of His return have received that witness in their spirit that He is returning very soon.

Because this is true, I can promise you this: "To begin with, you must know and understand this, that scoffers (mockers) will come in the last days with scoffing, [people who] walk after their own fleshly desires and say, 'Where is the promise of His coming? For since the forefathers fell asleep, all things have continued exactly as they did from the beginning of creation'" (2 Peter 3:3-4). If you've been a Christian for any length of time, you've probably heard someone say something like that. You may have even said it yourself.

THE MIDNIGHT HOUR

If you think it's crazy that only the father of the groom knows when the marriage is going to happen, then you better hold on to your hat. What I'm about to write next may sound even crazier. Scholars have found that in the Galilean wedding tradition, the announcement would be made at night. The father would wake the groom and the groomsmen and then tell him to get his bride. He would then blow a shofar or trumpet.

In Jesus' day the population of Nazareth was between 300-400 people. The blowing of the shofar or trumpet would likely wake up the entire town. Everyone would know that a wedding was going to take place. "But at midnight there was a shout, 'Behold, the bridegroom! Go out to meet him!'" (Matthew 25:6).

When the groom arrived at the home of the bride, the bride and her party would be ready because they would have heard the trumpet blast also. They would have so little time to get ready before the arrival of the groom that the entire bridal party would sleep in their wedding garments. Two of the groomsmen would provide a seat with a pole on either side, to carry her to her new home. This was referred to as "flying the bride to the Father's house." It was here at the father's house that the marriage supper took place.

This is such a beautiful foreshadowing of the Marriage Supper of the Lamb which the Apostle John wrote about in Revelation 19:7-8: "Let us rejoice and shout for joy [exulting and triumphant]! Let us celebrate and ascribe to Him glory and honor, for the marriage of the Lamb [at last] has come, and His bride has prepared herself. She has been permitted to dress in fine (radiant) linen, dazzling and white— for the fine linen is (signifies, represents) the righteousness (the upright, just, and godly living, deeds, and conduct, and right standing with God) of the saints (God's holy people)."

IMPORTANCE OF PROPHECY

THE WEDDING GARMENTS

When I read "the fine linen is the righteous deeds of the saints," the thought came to my mind, *could it be that some wedding garments will be more glorious than others at the Marriage Supper of the Lamb, as part of their reward?* It only makes sense to me as I think of weddings here in America. Every little girl dreams of her wedding day and dreams of how beautiful it will be. Some brides come from wealthy families, or have amassed wealth on their own, and so their choice of a wedding dress isn't limited by the cost.

That naturally made me think about the most expensive wedding dress ever. Out of the top ten ever recorded, number 10 was a measly one million dollars. Number 1, [Are you ready for this?], was thirty million dollars. WOW! I know right now many of you are going to stop reading, do a search to see what they looked like, and find out how they could be so expensive.

Others have come from poor circumstances and were only able to afford a very modest wedding dress, or none at all. If you are the latter, I have some great news for you if the quality of our wedding garment is part of our reward.

Jesus said, "Do not gather and heap up and store up for yourselves treasures on earth, where moth and rust and worm consume and destroy, and where thieves break through and steal. But gather and heap up and store for yourselves treasures in heaven, where neither moth nor rust nor worm consume and destroy, and where thieves do not break through and steal; for where your treasure is, there will your heart be also" (Matthew 6:19-21). We can send treasure on ahead of us to heaven. The more devoted you are to the Lord and the harder you work to build His Kingdom; the greater will be your reward and greater the treasure.

HOPE CHEST

Paul was giving Titus, as a younger pastor, instructions on what to teach those in his church on how to live a holy and righteous life. One of the main incentives he uses is we are, " Awaiting and looking for the [fulfillment, the realization of our] blessed hope, even the glorious appearing of our great God and Savior Christ Jesus (the Messiah, the Anointed One)" (Titus 2:13 NASB).

Because I'm a man, this thought never crossed my mind before until writing about these events. Speaking of the blessed hope in this context, caused me to think of what many girls had in my day, which was a hope chest. I don't know if they still have those or not.

A hope chest was traditionally given to the oldest daughter in the family, and as she collected special items for her future wedding, she would store them in this chest. It was also referred to as a glory box, a dowry chest, or a bridal trousseau.

Just think about it ladies and dream a little. Your heavenly Father has unlimited wealth. Based on what you do while here on earth, you can store up treasure in heaven for your heavenly wedding dress that will make that 30-million-dollar dress pale in comparison.

There is an excitement building within me because of what I believe is the headline coming out of heaven's newsrooms. My imagination being what it is, I see huge monitors all throughout heaven flashing the news, reminiscent of headlines in ancient Galilee of an approaching wedding: "JESUS, SON OF DAVID, HAS COMPLETED THE ROOM ADDITIONS! BETTER GET READY! WE'RE GOING TO HAVE A WEDDING!"

CHAPTER 16

OUR INHERITANCE AND REWARDS

"The highest reward for a person's toil is not what they get for it, but what they become by it."

—John Ruskin

There are two judgments in the Bible that I mentioned earlier, in chapters 9 & 10. There is the Great White Throne Judgment in Revelation 20:11-15. This judgment occurs at the end of human history on this earth. It's at this judgment that the earth and sky (heaven) will be uncreated. They will no longer exist. If you appear before this judgment your eternal future will have already been decided. You will be spending eternity in hell.

"And just as it is appointed and destined for all men to die once and after this [comes certain] judgment" (Hebrews 9:27). Based on this verse I believe the first thing that will happen to us after the rapture of the Church is believers will stand before the Judgment Seat of Christ. As a refresher, I would like to quote again this judgment described in 2 Corinthians 5:10: "For we must all appear and be revealed as we are before the judgment seat of Christ, so that each one may receive [his pay] according to what he has done in the body, whether good or evil [considering what his purpose and motive have been, and what he has achieved, been busy with, and given himself and his attention to accomplishing]."

The future of those who appear before this judgment will have already been decided as well. They will spend eternity in heaven. This judgment is to decide what kind of rewards we will receive from the Master.

There are a couple of more rewards that I would like to mention here that I didn't mention in Chapter 9. I saved them for now so that they will be fresh in your memory as we enter Chapter 17.

OUR INHERITANCE

When I was much younger we used to sing an old hymn titled "I've Got a Mansion Just over the Hilltop." When we think of mansions here on earth, we think of some massive estate that only the wealthiest can afford. Children of the wealthy generally receive these estates as their inheritance.

Remember what Jesus told the disciples in John 15:2 (NASB)? "In My Father's house are many rooms; if that were not so, I would have told you, because I am going there to prepare a place for you." We will

OUR INHERITANCE AND REWARDS

have a room in the Father's house with Him. It can't get any better than that. If, as the old hymn says, Jesus is building us a mansion it would not even compare, no matter how large and nice, to the Father's house. Throughout eternity we are all going to live together as one big happy family. There won't be any family squabbles nor will there be any irritating relatives to put a damper on our joy.

I believe another part of our inheritance is what God told the prophet Ezekiel that Israel's inheritance will be. God Himself will be our inheritance along with our ministry to Him. "This [their ministry to Me] shall be to them as an inheritance, for I am their inheritance; and you shall give them no possession in Israel, for I am their possession." Does that blow your mind or what? We will inherit God!

Kings of old appointed people in their kingdoms to positions of authority based on how loyal they were to them. In the same way, as I am writing this, President-elect Trump is selecting members for his important cabinet positions. His most loyal supporters, defenders, and followers, if approved, will be rewarded with the highest positions in his administration.

I have a Christian friend, quite successful in real estate, who was not excited about heaven. He thought we would be sitting on a cloud strumming a harp throughout eternity. I wouldn't blame him for not being excited if this were true. Eternity would be really boring to say the least. I wouldn't be excited about that either. Think of the most exciting, fun, and fulfilling experiences you've ever had in your life—they won't come close to what eternity in heaven will be like.

I have been envious of people whose jobs were their dream jobs. They wake up every day excited to go to work because they love what they do. They're not that excited about retirement. Many will do it right up to the day they die.

Whether we receive great rewards (high positions of authority), or small rewards in his kingdom, whatever our ministry to him, we will absolutely love it. It will be our dream job! Jesus said we were created to do good works. He also said it is more blessed to give than to receive.

In light of what Jesus said, what do you think the greatest reward will be for those he is the most pleased with? He actually tells us what the greatest in His kingdom will do in Matthew 23:11: "He who is greatest among you shall be your servant."

My friend in real estate was my mentor. Whenever I had a problem, or needed advice, I knew I could go to him. He never once complained even though I called on him often. He loved helping others to succeed. He lived out the truth that it is more blessed to give than to receive. As a result, everybody loved and respected him.

When the Lord blesses me and the Holy Spirit reveals truths to me in the Word, the greatest joys I have experienced is when I can share those blessing and insights with others. My hope is that I can share my blessings and rewards with many others in heaven throughout eternity, making heaven that much more enjoyable for them and for me.

REWARDS

I have been blessed to read through the Bible many times and one thing that really piques my interest is the difference between humans here on earth and heavenly beings. Let's look at some of those passages describing angels and their appearance. When angels appeared to humans in scripture they had an otherworldly appearance. The writers struggled with how to describe them in human terms and often used the word "like."

When the Archangel Gabriel was sent to deliver a message to Daniel he was delayed for three weeks by the prince of Persia, who was likely a demon spirit that had authority over the Kingdom of Persia. The Archangel Michael came to Gabriel's aid which freed him to deliver his message.

Gabriel is referred to as a man in this passage. "I lifted up my eyes and looked, and behold, a man clothed in linen, whose loins were girded with pure gold of Uphaz. His body also was [a golden luster] like beryl, his face had the appearance of lightning, his eyes were like flaming torches, his arms and his feet like glowing burnished bronze, and the sound of his words was like the noise of a multitude [of people or the roaring of the sea]" (Daniel 10:5-6). When Daniel saw him he was so terrified he fainted and fell face down in the dirt. Although there is no description of Michael's appearance in the Bible, I'm sure he is just as amazing and terrifying in person as Gabriel.

In Ezekiel 1:5-7 we have described for us the appearance of cherubim. "And out of the midst of it came the likeness of four living creatures [or cherubim]. And this was their appearance: they had the likeness of a man, but each one had four faces and each one had four wings. And their legs were straight legs, and the sole of their feet was like the sole of a calf's foot, and they sparkled like burnished bronze."

But there were times when angels appeared in human form. That's why the writer to the Hebrews wrote this: "Do not neglect hospitality to strangers, for by this some have entertained angels without knowing it" (Hebrews 13:2 NASB).

DRESSING GOD

In Ezekiel 28:13 we have the description of Lucifer (Satan) before he fell and was cast out of heaven. "You were in Eden, the garden of God; every precious stone was your covering, the carnelian, topaz, jasper, chrysolite, beryl, onyx, sapphire, carbuncle, and emerald; and your settings and your sockets and engravings were wrought in gold. On the day that you were created they were prepared." He was a creature of immense beauty and his heart was lifted up in pride.

Another example of the difference between heavenly beings and earthly beings is found in Revelation 18:1. "Then I saw another angel descending from heaven, possessing great authority, and the earth was illuminated with his radiance and splendor."

These angelic beings are awesome creatures in light of how they are described by various writers, but I saved the best for last, Jesus Christ. When Jesus was on this earth the prophet Isaiah in Isaiah 53:2 (NASB) described him this way: "For He grew up before Him like a tender shoot, and like a root out of dry ground; He has no stately form or majesty that we would look at Him, nor an appearance that we would take pleasure in Him."

But when he is seen in His glorified body, it's a whole different story. John, in Revelation 1:14-15, describes him thus: "His head and His hair were white like white wool, [as white] as snow, and His eyes [flashed] like a flame of fire. His feet glowed like burnished (bright) bronze as it is refined in a furnace, and His voice was like the sound of many waters."

You might think I've gone off the deep end with what I'm about to say, but I actually think this could be one of our rewards. As awesome as angels are, we might be even more glorious in our immortal, glorified bodies. "Beloved, we are [even here and] now God's children;

OUR INHERITANCE AND REWARDS

it is not yet disclosed (made clear) what we shall be [hereafter], but we know that when He comes and is manifested, we shall [as God's children] resemble and be like Him, for we shall see Him just as He [really] is" (1 John 3:2).

Could it be that when we get to heaven our appearance, like Christ's, will be changed into something far more glorious? Do you remember the story of Moses when he was on Mount Sinai for forty days, receiving the Ten Commandments from God? What did it say about Moses' appearance? "Moses came down from Mount Sinai, carrying the two tablets with God's words on them. His face was shining from speaking with the Lord but he didn't know it. When Aaron and all the Israelites looked at Moses and saw his face shining, they were afraid to come near him" (Exodus 34:29-30). Does that sound familiar?

What happened? "Then Moses said, 'Please let me see your glory'" (Exodus 33:18). For a brief, passing moment, Moses saw the glory of the Lord and his face shone. Can you imagine the effect that being in the very presence of God for all eternity will have on our appearance? The more Christ-like we are here on this earth, the more like Christ we will be when we are in His presence.

Speaking of Jesus, the writer to the Hebrews said, "For some little time You have ranked him lower than and inferior to the angels; You have crowned him with glory and honor and set him over the works of Your hands" (Hebrews 2:7).

Just like Christ we are now "lower than and inferior to the angels," but through Christ's work of atonement on the cross we have become "heirs of God and fellow heirs with Christ [sharing His inheritance with Him]" (Romans 8:17).

Just one more quote from Scripture to suggest my imagination might have some validity. "And the teachers and those who are wise shall shine like the brightness of the firmament, and those who turn many to righteousness (to uprightness and right standing with God) [shall give forth light] like the stars forever and ever" (Daniel 12:3). We will be like glistening jewels in God's crown. Beautiful, shimmering, immortal beings surrounding His throne forever, worshipping the One who crowned us with His glory.

I was so excited when the Holy Spirit brought these Scriptures to my attention. There are those special occasions when the Holy Spirit reveals some truth to you that you've never understood before. I like describing it as a verse of passage from the Bible leaping off the page into my heart.

In all the years I have been in church I had never heard anyone else mention these scriptures, suggesting that our appearance might be so drastically changed as part of our reward. Nobody wants to be considered a nutcase, but I felt strongly that the Holy Spirit led me to these scriptures and to these conclusions. I felt so much better about my conclusions when I was made aware of what I considered to be supporting evidence by a second witness. Sometime later I purchased the book *Heaven*, by Randy Alcorn (I highly recommend this book for those desiring to learn more about heaven), and learned that he thought that might be a possibility as well.

CHAPTER 17

MARRIAGE SUPPER OF THE LAMB

"I found him whom my soul loves."

—SONG OF SOLOMON 3:4

Paul tells us of something coming in the near future which should create growing excitement in us who are awaiting His return. "For you yourselves know perfectly well that the day of the [return of the] Lord will come [as unexpectedly and suddenly] as a thief in the night" (1 Thessalonians 5:2).

Along with this verse we must not leave out the verse which relates to everyone being awakened from their sleep. "For we say this to you by the word of the Lord, that we who are alive and remain until the coming of the Lord will not precede those who have fallen asleep. For the Lord Himself will descend from heaven with a shout, with the voice of the archangel and with the trumpet of God, and the dead in Christ will rise first. Then we who are alive, who remain, will be caught up together with them in the clouds to meet the Lord in the air, and so we will always be with the Lord" (1 Thessalonians 4:15-17).

Just like the imagery of the villagers awakened from their sleep, so will those "who have previously fallen asleep" (died) be awakened when the trumpet sounds and a shout shakes the heavens as our Bridegroom comes for His Bride.

Do you remember me mentioning earlier that many people have a mental picture of Jesus never raising his voice? Could people have this mindset because of what Isaiah wrote concerning the Messiah? "He will not cry or shout aloud or cause His voice to be heard in the street" (Isaiah 42:2). I'm sure I'm like most everyone else in that I didn't know where to find it, but I remembered the basics of what it said.

Our problem is that we can often remember the basics of a scripture, but we do not know the context in which it was written. What Isaiah was saying is that Jesus wouldn't be like so many, who, wanting to make a name for themselves, try to attract and hold people's interest and attention. That certainly wasn't Jesus. He quietly went about his Father's business.

But that wasn't always the case. Do you remember when He shouted life into a dead man? "He shouted with a loud voice, Lazarus, come out!" (John 11:43).

If he shouted then, we ain't [sic] heard nothing yet. There's coming a time in the near future when He's going to shout so loud it will raise millions from the dead. Referring back to 1 Thessalonians 4 above it says, "For the Lord Himself will descend from heaven with a shout."

WEDDING DAY IN HEAVEN

The wedding day has finally arrived. Let the celebration begin! Revelation 19:6: "After that I heard what sounded like the shout of a vast throng, like the boom of many pounding waves, and like the roar of terrific and mighty peals of thunder." There may be many of you reading this that grew up in traditional churches. You may be used to people speaking in whispers while in church, very calmly singing, none of this jumping up and down, dancing, clapping, and even shouting, as you've seen in what you might consider weird churches. The thought might have even crossed your mind that that's just emotional manipulation by the pastor or worship leader.

If you are used to a staid church setting, heaven may come as a big shock to you. When Jesus presents Himself at the Marriage Supper of the Lamb, according to John, we are going to be beside ourselves with excitement. All of that and more. God gives us immortal bodies that cannot be destroyed because when we see Him and experience the glories of heaven, if we were in our earthly bodies we would be in sensory overload.

If you are uncomfortable clapping your hands in church, or raising your hands in worship, or expressing your emotions of joy through shouting, or God forbid, dancing in church; you may be a little bit in dread of that day. But you don't have to worry, it will happen as naturally as breathing.

A DESTINATION WEDDING

Over the centuries there have been many different types of weddings. There are the traditional weddings steeped in customs and rituals. Or maybe you would prefer a beach wedding where the toes of the participants are bathed in warm black sand; the backdrop is beautiful blue ocean as far as the eye can see; the sound of seagulls flying overhead; and the sound of the ocean waves coming ashore. Another could be a garden wedding with the backdrop of beautiful flowers amidst lush greenery.

And then there is the destination wedding. Put your imagination in gear and imagine you have a billionaire dad who tells you he will pay for the entire wedding, with no limit to the number of guests. Everyone's travel, accommodations, and food expenses included for a whole week. Now think of the most incredible destination in the world. Wouldn't that be awesome!

As awesome as that would be, it would be like you were having your wedding in a garbage dump compared to the destination wedding in store for us who have put our faith in Christ as our Lord and Savior. Our future wedding destination is out of this world!

When does our future wedding celebration happen? Shortly after the rapture of the Church, the Bride of Christ. "Take notice! I tell you a mystery (a secret truth, an event decreed by the hidden purpose or counsel of God). We shall not all fall asleep [in death], but we shall all be changed (transformed). In a moment, in the twinkling of an eye, at the [sound of the] last trumpet call. For a trumpet will sound, and the dead [in Christ] will be raised imperishable (free and immune from decay), and we shall be changed (transformed)" (1 Corinthians 15:51-52).

MARRIAGE SUPPER OF THE LAMB

One moment we are inhabiting a weak, frail body of flesh, and then suddenly we are clothed with an immortal, indestructible body and we meet Christ in the air. Once gathered there with him, He then takes us to heaven.

After we appear before the judgment seat of Christ for the works we have done while on earth we're told it's time to party. While the people on earth are going through the Great Tribulation for seven years, we are going to be at the Marriage Supper of the Lamb for seven years. Now that's what I call a party.

Picture this setting. The angels have ushered us into the wedding banquet attended by billions of saints. Using my creative thinking, I envision the banqueting hall is like the largest colosseum you can imagine. Rows and rows of tables as far as the eye can see, looking down on the colosseum floor. Your angel, an incredible and awesome being, leads you to your table where you take a seat and he informs you as the Bride you can choose the menu. I would personally suggest you ask him what the groom is having, seeing as how you have never eaten of heaven's food before.

While you are sitting there waiting for the festivities to begin, those around you are complimenting you on your new appearance. Comments such as, "You look so much like Christ!" Or, "What kind of jewels are those on your robe? They are so beautiful. I've never seen anything like them before." In the meantime, you are saying some of the very same things about them.

As you look around, as far as the eye can see, are an innumerable host of glorified saints indescribable in beauty, everyone having a different and unique appearance. Suddenly the door on the floor of the colosseum opens and you pinch yourself to make sure you're awake and not just dreaming. Who is it you ask? It's none other than the famous Bible characters that we had read about during our life on earth.

Even though we have never seen them, somehow we immediately know who they are. Noah, Abraham, Moses, Ruth, David, Esther, Daniel, Mary (the mother of Jesus), and Joseph, the twelve apostles, and Paul. Plus, many more from throughout history. They proceed to the head table, which is massive, to take their places of honor, but because there are so many people gathered together, the head table is literally a mile away from where you are sitting.

You're first reaction reading this, because you're a mile away, is probably, "That stinks!" But don't forget—you're the bride of the groom and the bride always gets the best seat at the wedding banquet. If you are wondering how that can be, the answer is simple. It's heaven. Somehow, it seems everyone there has the best seat in the house. Your view will be unobstructed, and now that you are immortal, your vision and hearing will be such that it will seem like you are actually sitting right across the table from the Bible person you wanted to meet the most.

All of heaven is buzzing with excitement and the noise is building to a crescendo. Your senses are being bombarded in an incredible way that is incomprehensible. Just when you think you can't stand any more excitement, the angel Gabriel appears at the door and announces the groom's arrival. In case you aren't sure who that is, it's Jesus!

Suddenly it's so quiet that you could hear the proverbial pin drop. And then the room explodes with the sound of billions of saints, overwhelmed with joy, shouting their praises as Jesus enters the room! Never has there been a sound heard like that in all creation.

"After that I heard what sounded like the shout of a vast throng, like the boom of many pounding waves, and like the roar of terrific and mighty peals of thunder, exclaiming, Hallelujah (praise the Lord)! For now the Lord our God the Omnipotent (the All-Ruler) reigns! Let us rejoice and shout for joy [exulting and triumphant]! Let us celebrate and ascribe to Him glory and honor, for the marriage of the Lamb [at last] has come, and His bride has prepared herself" (Revelation 19:6-7).

As joyous, happy, excited, and thrilled as we will be when we see Jesus, it won't even come close to His display of joy when His Bride is finally with Him on that day.

Here's my feeble attempt at describing what happens when Jesus enters the colosseum. His love, joy, and delight in us emanates from Him like a massive tsunami wave, roaring from the colosseum floor to the furthest expanse of those gathered there. Left in its wake are myriads of saints, overwhelmed by an indescribable depth of emotions of joy, love, and adoration, lying flat on their faces in worship.

His love is infinite and perfect, lacking nothing. There is no way we can comprehend how that infinite love will be expressed on that day. I do know this though—it will be beyond compare.

THE WEDDING CELEBRATION

In considering wedding receptions down here on earth there are certain activities involved. What follows may not be the customs where you are from, but these are the ones I'm familiar with. Great food and drink. There may be music and dancing. And for the really rich and famous there may be world-renowned singers and musicians.

And then of course there are the speeches from the groomsmen and the bridesmaids.

To say the food at Jesus's reception will be great is an understatement. Generally, after everyone's been served their food, and while we are eating, the men and women at the head table will give their speeches. [There will be no groomsmen and bridesmaids at Jesus's reception because we are all the Bride of Christ.]

Just like the groomsmen here on earth, they will tell wonderful stories of life experiences they had with our heavenly groom, Jesus. Who would be in your lineup? Maybe Jesus would have those in the Old Testament speak first. Who better to start than Adam, the first man. [This is just my natural man speaking, but I think he might want to do some apologizing.] Following him might be Noah. Then Abraham, Issac, Jacob, Moses, David, Isaiah, etc. I feel terrible leaving anyone out, but Jesus will take care of that.

When we get to the New Testament speakers, Paul, for me, would be a good starter. Then Peter. James and John might be like a tag team. And then as many as the Lord would have speak. I mean, we do have seven years. The one to end it on the men's side may be Joseph, Jesus' earthly father.

If the order stays the same for the women, then it would naturally follow that Eve would be the first to speak. [Yes, I'm thinking the same thing about Eve as I was about Adam.] Sarah, the wife of Abraham. Rahab, the great, great, great, grandmother of King David. Ruth, the grandmother of David. Then Hannah, the mother of Samuel. Maybe to finish the women from the Old Testament, Queen Esther.

Starting in the New Testament lineup for the women would be someone you've possibly never heard of. According to Christian tradition, Anne was the mother of Mary, the mother of Jesus. I would like to hear the thoughts of the mother of a virgin giving birth to a child. Then there's Anna, the prophetess in the temple when Mary and Joseph bring Jesus to the temple for consecration when, upon seeing him, begins to proclaim the arrival of Israel's Messiah. Mary Magdalene. Mary and Martha might be a tag team like James and John. Then there's Priscilla, co-laborer with Aquila. Dorcas whom Jesus raised from the dead. And last, but certainly not least, Mary, the earthly mother of Jesus.

Have you ever listened to someone speaking and you were disappointed when they concluded? If those speeches were to actually happen, I can guarantee this, you wouldn't want them to ever stop. You may be surprised, but there are still two speakers who know Jesus better than anyone. I've saved the best and the greatest, they are unequaled, no one even comes close, for last. God, the Holy Spirit, who empowered Jesus during his earthly ministry. And the keynote speaker—God, the Father of the Groom—and our heavenly matchmaker. "No one is able to come to Me unless the Father Who sent Me attracts and draws him and gives him the desire to come to Me" (John 6:44 AMPC).

LET THE RECEPTION BEGIN

And now let the singing, the music, and the dancing begin. Naturally, Jesus would want the greatest singer of all time to sing at his reception—none other than God the Father. And for His backup singers and musicians he has a host of angels. WHAT??!! That's right! Here's scripture to back it up.

"The Lord your God is in the midst of you, a Mighty One, a Savior [Who saves]! He will rejoice over you with joy; He will rest [in silent satisfaction] and in His love He will be silent and make no mention [of past sins, or even recall them]; He will exult over you with singing" (Zephaniah 3:17 MSG). My imagination being what it is I'm sure there will be some songs where the Holy Spirit will join Him.

Jesus will be too busy to join in the singing because He will be totally focused on dancing with His Bride. Yes, I believe I have scriptural evidence for that as well. The Bible tells us that David was a man after God's own heart. What is the most famous story of David throwing a party? It was when he brought the Ark of the Covenant into Jerusalem. "And David danced before the Lord with all his might, clad in a linen ephod" [a priest's upper garment] (2 Samuel 6:14).

If David was a man after God's own heart, then God must love dancing. Why wouldn't Jesus be dancing at His own wedding reception? Everyone knows the groom always has a special dance with his bride. Most of the time, here on earth, it's a slow dance. I don't believe that's going to be the case at this wedding reception. The Bride (you and me), and the Groom will be filled with so much joy we will be dancing with all of our might.

All of heaven will be filled with the songs of God the Father and of the Holy Spirit, and Jesus and His Bride will be dancing like there's no tomorrow, because there won't be. Here on earth, there may not be a tomorrow for us because we may die. But on that day in heaven, we will be immortal, and eternity for us will have just begun. It will be one continuous day forever.

CHAPTER 18

UNSPEAKABLE JOY AND FULL OF GLORY

The joy of the Lord is your strength and stronghold.

—NEHEMIAH 8:10

I feel the need to build on this truth that many have never associated with Jesus—joy. Some people, when they think of Jesus, they think of the verse of Scripture that says, "He was despised and rejected by men, a Man of sorrows and pain and acquainted with grief; and like One from whom men hide their faces He was despised, and we did not appreciate His worth or esteem Him" (Isaiah 53:3).

Others, when thinking of Him, see Him as someone quiet, solemn, serious, never cracking a smile. I don't believe anything could be further from the truth. As a matter of fact, Jesus's enemies accused Him, in today's vernacular, of being a party animal. "The Son of Man came eating and drinking, and they say, 'Here is a glutton and a drunkard, a friend of tax collectors and sinners'" (Matthew 11:19). In their opinion He was having too much fun, and hanging out with the wrong crowd.

In Luke 15 Jesus tells the parable of the Lost Coin. When the woman finds the coin she lost, she calls her friends to come and celebrate with her because she found what she had lost. And then He says this, "In the same way, I tell you, there is joy in the presence of the angels of God over one sinner who repents" (Luke 15:10 NASB).

In the past when I read this, my thoughts were on the angels celebrating over one sinner who repents. But I realized in the parable the focus is on the woman who lost the coin, not the friends and neighbors who helped her celebrate. The one who celebrates the most is our Savior who has recovered the lost soul. And since there are thousands around the world everyday who repent, He's having a party 24/7, 365 days a year.

We just covered the Parable of The Ten Virgins which ended in a grand party. Immediately following that, Jesus tells the Parable of the Talents. It's the story of a man going away on a long journey, who calls his servants, giving each one a part of his property to manage. After a long time away, he returned and required his servants to give an account of how they handled his money. The first two servants doubled the amount they received. This is what their master said to them, "Enter into and share the joy (the delight, the blessedness) which your master enjoys" (Matthew 25:23).

UNSPEAKABLE JOY AND FULL OF GLORY

Jesus relates these parables to Himself and the main emphasis in all three is on joy. He wants us to enter into, experience, and share His joy.

Consider this verse: "You will show me the path of life; in Your presence is fullness of joy, at Your right hand there are pleasures forevermore" (Psalm 16:11). Formerly, when reading this verse, I was guilty of being focused on myself and what I feel in those times when I'm in His presence. There have been some special times when I have had a strong sense of His presence and "I experienced" a unique joy. If you've ever experienced His presence, you know what I'm talking about. But sadly, those times come to an end, and it leaves me wanting more.

The first and last part of this verse is not focused on us, but on God. "He shows us" the path of life. It's about Him. "At His right hand" there are pleasures forevermore. Again, it's about Him. Good hermeneutics tells us that the middle part of the verse, "in His presence is fullness of joy," is about Him as well.

The Hebrew word translated "fullness" carries with it the implication of being "fully satisfied." In other words, there's nothing lacking. Nothing more needs to be added. Because God is infinite, His joy is infinite—He never has more and He never has less, He's got it all. When we are in His presence we experience "His joy." He's the One I want to hang out with for all eternity.

As I was writing this, a book came to mind: *All Quiet on the Western Front* by Erich Maria Remarque, a German veteran of World War I. It is a vivid portrayal of the brutalities of war, as well as the difficulties of soldiers reentering civilian life. Heaven is the extreme opposite of what is portrayed in that book. Heaven is filled with joy, laughter, and celebration, as weary warriors enter their eternal rest.

In Luke 21:26 (NASB), Jesus said in the last days, right before He returns, people's heart's will be "fainting from fear and the expectation of the things that are coming upon the world." As I see the last day events that Jesus spoke of unfolding right before my eyes, my emotions are in turmoil. I'm both troubled and saddened, that people aren't aware of where we are on God's timeline, because of the lack of teaching in many churches. Their hearts are filled with anxiety as they see the world falling apart before their eyes.

But my heart is also overflowing with joy, knowing that very soon Jesus will be coming for His Bride, and I can hardly wait. That kind of joy will get us through what may be difficult days ahead for us. We can have that joy because we have read the end of the book, and we know we are going to win.

CHAPTER 19

THE REST OF THE STORY

Some of you that are older may recognize this title from a radio program originally hosted by Paul Harvey. Mr. Harvey would tell interesting stories on a variety of subjects, while holding back some key element of the story. Usually, they were about famous people. As he told the story you would be trying to figure out who the person was. At the end of the broadcast after revealing who it was, he would famously say in his own inimitable way, "And now you know—the rest of the story."

I would like to finish by telling you the story of a famous person who was an impersonator. This will be my weak attempt to imitate Paul Harvey. This person lived in upstate New York, ran away from home when his parents separated, and ended up in New York City. He started out by writing fraudulent checks and as he gained confidence he moved on to much grander schemes.

He claimed to have worked as an assistant state attorney general in the state of Louisiana; served as a hospital physician in Georgia; impersonated a Pan Am airline pilot who logged over 2 million miles; eventually spending time in prison in France, later extradited to Sweden to serve time in prison there, and then later extradited to the United States to spend time in a federal prison. While in the federal penitentiary, he escaped three times—one time masquerading as a prison inspector, walking out the front door of the prison.

After serving his time, he founded a company, which advised companies on how to secure documents. His name was Frank Abagnale. A book was published about his life and was later turned into a movie by the same name, *Catch Me If You Can*. And now you know—the rest of the story.

That may have sounded like a glamorous, adrenaline-filled life. Not so, according to him. I watched an interview of him on the Johnny Carson show. He told Johnny that it was a lonely, stressful life, always on the run.

Why do I tell a story like this at the end of my book? The whole burden of this book is the fact that the Church is filled with impersonators. We, especially here in America, are like Frank in many ways. Not that we have succumbed to a life of crime, but we have become very adept as impersonators.

WHAT'S YOUR STORY?

I had wonderful parents, but some have been told by their parents, or someone significant in their life, that they will never amount to anything. Some have been told they're dumb and good for nothing. Others, "I wish you were never born," "you're a disappointment,"

THE REST OF THE STORY

"you look terrible," "too fat, too thin, too ugly, you don't have what it takes to get ahead in life."

So what happens many times when we've had these experiences? We believe the lies we've been told and go around trying to impersonate people who we think have it all together, by putting up a false front. We've all known people who have a bad self-image. You may even now have a close friend who struggles with feelings of worthlessness. Or worse yet, you may be that person. I would like to tell you a story that I hope will help you, or help you help a friend.

Before I met my wife, I was blessed to date some exceptionally beautiful, sweet, smart women. If you were to see me and hear me say that, you would probably say, "Yeah, right. That's your story and you're sticking to it."

My wife's late husband was a chiropractor, and we attended the same church. My wife loves to tell the story that one Sunday, she and her late husband were sitting in the balcony of the church, and he looked down and saw me come in with a gorgeous blonde. He turned to her and said, "How does Garry Harris get those tall, good-looking blondes to date him?" Obviously, he wasn't impressed with my looks. And why not? I was all of 5'8" and balding. So, she said, "Who's Garry Harris?" And he said, pointing to me, "He's that bald headed guy down there." Once she saw who he was speaking of, much to my chagrin when I hear her telling this story, she said, "I don't know."

For reasons which I will not go into, I always found a reason not to marry. By saying that, I'm not implying that all those beautiful women wanted to marry me. By the time I was in my mid-fifties I was pretty much over the dating scene. What good looks I had, if any, were fading rapidly. It was then I had an experience that changed me, and I hope will be helpful to those who've had negative things said to them throughout their lives.

One Sunday, the wife of a pastor on staff asked me, "Why don't you ask so-and-so out." The woman she was speaking of was another tall, beautiful blonde. (Just in case you're thinking, "You seem to think you're all that and a bag of chips," my wife, if asked, will confirm that she wasn't a figment of my imagination. She knows of whom I speak.) I responded by saying, "She's way out of my league." To which she replied, something to the effect, "If you have that mind-set you don't deserve to ask her out."

Well, when she said that I decided she was right. I needed to change my way of thinking. That pastor's wife still doesn't have a clue that what she said changed the course of my life for the better. I will explain that in a minute. But right now, I want to proudly say that a short time after that, probably before my courage receded, I ran into her and took the opportunity to ask her out. Surprise, surprise—she shot me down!

I later became aware of my wife through some mutual friends and needless to say, found her extremely attractive. To give you an idea of how pretty she is, after we were married, I found out that when she was much younger her friends thought she looked like Jaclyn Smith. I have now seen pictures of her when she was younger, and I can confirm that. Not so much now, only in the sense that when we were married, she was a brunette just like Jaclyn. Now after fourteen years living with me her hair is totally white. She's still beautiful, but I think living with me has been pretty hard on her, if her hair is any indication.

One morning in church, I was with a friend and pointed her out, commenting on how pretty she was. His response was the same as mine earlier, "Forget it buddy, she's way out of your league." But because I had that conversation with the pastor's wife, I ignored him. On the day we were married I became a husband, a dad to two wonderful children, and a granddad to two incredible grandchildren, all in one fell swoop. We now have six awesome grandchildren. And I must admit when I got her to say yes, I definitely outran my coverage.

Every once in a while, I think back to what my friend said that day, and I take great pleasure in reminding myself how wrong he was. And now you know—the rest of the story.

LIES AND SCARS

The reason I shared this story is there are some of you reading this now that have mental scars from things said and done to you in the past, which have kept you beaten down. Satan has convinced you that you will never overcome your past. You have bought into his lies. If you allow Him, Jesus can come in and set you free from your past.

Here are some of God's promises to you that I hope will change the way you view yourself:

> *"No weapon that is formed against you will succeed; and you will condemn every tongue that accuses you in judgment. This is the heritage of the servants of the Lord, and their vindication is from Me," declares the Lord"* (Isaiah 54:17 NASB).

> *"For I am the Lord your God who takes hold of your right hand, who says to you, 'Do not fear, I will help you'"* (Isaiah 41:13 NASB).

Any time your enemy tells you lies that you are not enough, quote this Scripture, "And He has said to me, 'My grace is sufficient for you, for power is perfected in weakness.' Most gladly, therefore, I will rather boast about my weaknesses, so that the power of Christ may dwell in me" (2 Corinthians 12:9 NASB). God has given us these, and many more promises, and when he makes a promise, he keeps it.

Lastly, some of you have bought into the lie that you are not worthy enough to be loved. I love this quote that I first heard from Pastor Lindell, "God doesn't love you because you are valuable, you are valuable because God loves you." This is a biblical truth based on Deuteronomy 7:7-8. It's not who we are that makes us valuable, but whose we are.

There are many examples of this in everyday life. A pair of Nike Air Jordan 1's owned by Michael Jordan sold for $560,000. Kim Kardashian paid $65,625 for a velvet jacket worn by Michael Jackson for her six-year-old daughter, North. Darth Vader's helmet worn by actor David Prowse in *Star Wars Episode V: the Empire Strikes Back* sold for $898,420. A General Lee 1969 Charger from *The Dukes of Hazard* sold for $9,900,500. A silver dog bowl owned by Joan Rivers sold for $13,750. And last but not least, because I love golf, the most expensive golf club ever sold at auction was owned by Tiger Woods, and sold at auction in August of 2021 for $393,300. The reason these items were so valuable is for the simple fact of who owned them.[53]

When Jesus Christ purchased our salvation with His precious blood, we who have accepted Christ as our Lord and Savior, became God the Father's most valuable possession. Because God is holy His justice demanded judgment of our sins. Jesus took our place and bore our judgment, so that we might be restored to the Father, thus making us His most valuable possession, because the price that was paid for us was the life of His only Begotten Son.

ANOTHER TEMPTATION TEMPLATE

None of us are surprised when our enemies will say and do things to make us weaker, so they can defeat us. But because Satan is the great deceiver, and the father of lies, he uses a tactic that catches many people off guard, thus gaining victory over them. This tactic has been the impetus driving me to author this book.

Here it is in a nutshell: "You are good enough." This is his second most effectively used template for temptation. Just like his first template "Did God really say _____?"—this temptation template has only four words, "You are good enough _____!" These templates many times are interchangeable.

Here are a few of his lies. [Preface each one with these words, with either: "You are good enough," or "Did God really say"]:

You're certainly much better than he or she is.

Your good works far outweigh the bad things you have done.

You are engaged to marry him or her so it's all right to sleep with them. In God's sight you are already married.

You don't need to go to church. It's just filled with a bunch of hypocrites.

The Bible says that there are none righteous, no, not even one. A scientific study done in 2012 supposedly refutes that statement. Here's the headline of the article: *"Scientists Probe Human Nature—and Discover We Are Good, After All."*[54]

"You're worthy because you are born and because you are here. Your being here, your being alive makes worthiness your birthright. You alone are enough." —Oprah Winfrey

We're all sinners. We're all going to make mistakes. Just accept it—He understands. (Even though you are continually living in or giving into sin.)

Our first and only standard is the Bible. It has stood the test of time. Here is one of many scriptures that address the lies above. "O Lord, the God of Israel, You are rigidly just and righteous, for we are left a remnant that is escaped, as it is this day. Behold, we are before You in our guilt, for none can stand before You because of this" (Ezra 9:15).

NO COMPROMISE

"A compromise is a situation in which people accept something slightly different from what they really want, because of circumstances or because they are considering the wishes of other people."[55]

Another word for "uncompromisingly" is "rigidly." The world says that we must be willing to compromise, but they have expanded the definition to mean we must also "approve" of an action even when we know it's evil. If we are going to be like Christ then we need to have the mind of Christ (1 Corinthians 2:16), and the same attitude of Christ that we will make no allowance for, no room for, and give no permission to the enemy to lead us away from Christ, by giving in, or even giving a moment's notice to unrighteous, unholy thoughts, desires, or actions.

The way we gain victory over the devil's temptations is through submission and resistance. "Submit therefore to God. But resist the devil, and he will flee from you" (James 4:7, NASB).

NO EXCUSES

As already stated, if you find yourself standing before the Great White Throne Judgment at the end of the ages (Revelation 20:11), your destiny is already decided. You will be spending eternity in hell. Any excuse you offer that day will not change things. "But God, I thought you would understand." "I had no choice. That's the way you made me." "But God, the Bible said that you're a God of infinite mercy." "I know the Bible said that we needed to make that decision while we were on earth, but surely you wouldn't send me to an eternal hell. That wouldn't be fair."

> *"Remember our history, friends, and be warned. All our ancestors were led by the providential Cloud and taken miraculously through the Sea. They went through the waters, in a baptism like ours, as Moses led them from enslaving death to salvation life. They all ate and drank identical food and drink, meals provided daily by God. They drank from the Rock, God's fountain for them that stayed with them wherever they were. And the Rock was Christ. But just experiencing God's wonder and grace didn't seem to mean much—most of them were defeated by temptation during the hard times in the desert, and God was not pleased.*
>
> *"The same thing could happen to us. We must be on guard so that we never get caught up in wanting our own way as they did. And we must not turn our religion into a circus as*

they did—'First the people partied, then they threw a dance.' We must not be sexually promiscuous—they paid for that, remember, with 23,000 deaths in one day! We must never try to get Christ to serve us instead of us serving him; they tried it, and God launched an epidemic of poisonous snakes. We must be careful not to stir up discontent; discontent destroyed them.

"These are all warning markers—danger!—in our history books, written down so that we don't repeat their mistakes. Our positions in the story are parallel—they at the beginning, we at the end—and we are just as capable of messing it up as they were. Don't be so naive and self-confident. You're not exempt. You could fall flat on your face as easily as anyone else. Forget about self-confidence; it's useless. Cultivate God-confidence.

"No test or temptation that comes your way is beyond the course of what others have had to face. All you need to remember is that God will never let you down; he'll never let you be pushed past your limit; he'll always be there to help you come through it.

"So, my very dear friends, when you see people reducing God to something they can use or control, get out of their company as fast as you can" (1 Corinthians 10:1-14, MSG).

"So, if you're serious about living this new resurrection life with Christ, act like it. Pursue the things over which Christ presides. Don't shuffle along, eyes to the ground, absorbed with the things right in front of you. Look up and be alert to what is

THE REST OF THE STORY

going on around Christ—that's where the action is. See things from his perspective.

"Your old life is dead. Your new life, which is your real life—even though invisible to spectators—is with Christ in God. He is your life. When Christ (your real life, remember) shows up again on this earth, you'll show up, too—the real you, the glorious you. Meanwhile, be content with obscurity, like Christ.

"And that means killing off everything connected with that way of death: sexual promiscuity, impurity, lust, doing whatever you feel like whenever you feel like it, and grabbing whatever attracts your fancy. That's a life shaped by things and feelings instead of by God. It's because of this kind of thing that God is about to explode in anger. It wasn't long ago that you were doing all that stuff and not knowing any better. But you know better now, so make sure it's all gone for good: bad temper, irritability, meanness, profanity, dirty talk.

"Don't lie to one another. You're done with that old life. It's like a filthy set of ill-fitting clothes you've stripped off and put in the fire. Now you're dressed in a new wardrobe. Every item of your new way of life is custom made by the Creator, with his label on it. All the old fashions are now obsolete.

"So, chosen by God for this new life of love, dress in the wardrobe God picked out for you: compassion, kindness, humility, quiet strength, discipline. Be even-tempered, content with second place, quick to forgive an offense. Forgive as quickly and completely as the Master forgave you. And regardless of what else you put on, wear love. It's your

basic, all-purpose garment. Never be without it" (Colossians 3:1-10,12-14, MSG).

"May God himself, the God who makes everything holy and whole, make you holy and whole, put you together—spirit, soul, and body—and keep you fit for the coming of our Master, Jesus Christ. The One who called you is completely dependable. If he said it, he'll do it!" (1 Thessalonians 5:23-24 MSG).

In closing let this be your prayer: *"Let not those who wait and hope and look for You, O Lord of hosts, be put to shame through me; let not those who seek and inquire for and require You [as their vital necessity] be brought to confusion and dishonor through me, O God of Israel"* (Psalm 69:6).

Finally, remind yourself every day, if need be, of this truth: "for His divine power has granted to us everything pertaining to life and godliness, through the true knowledge of Him who called us by His own glory and excellence" (2 Peter 1:3 NASB).

EPILOGUE

IF JESUS CAME TO YOUR HOUSE
by Lois Blanchard Eades

If Jesus came to your house to spend a day or two,
If He came unexpectedly, I wonder what you'd do?

Oh, I know you'd give your nicest room to such an honored Guest,
And all the food you'd serve Him would be the very best.
And you would keep assuring Him you're glad to have Him there,
That serving Him in your home is a joy beyond compare!

But when you saw Him coming, would you meet
Him at the door,
With arms outstretched in "welcome" to your heavenly Visitor?

Or would you have to change your clothes before you let Him in?
Or hide some magazines and put the Bible where they had been?

DRESSING GOD

Would you turn off the radio and TV and hope He hadn't heard?
Or wish you hadn't uttered that last, loud, hasty word?

Would you hide your worldly music and put some hymn books out?
Could you let Jesus walk right in, or would you rush about?

And I wonder—if the Savior spent a day or two with you,
Would you go right on doing the things you always do?

Would you keep right on saying the things you always say?
Would your life continue as it does from day to day?
Would your family conversation keep up its usual pace?
And would you find it hard each meal to say a table grace?

Would you sing the songs you always sing, and read the books you now read?
And let Him know all the things on which your mind and spirit feed?

Would you take Jesus with you everywhere you'd planned to go?
Or would you, maybe change your plans for just a day or so?

Would you be glad to have Him meet your very closest friends?
Or would you hope they stay away until His visit ends?

Would you be glad to have Him stay forever on and on?
Or would you sigh with great relief when He at last was gone?

It might be interesting to know the things that you would do,
If Jesus came in person to spend some time with you.

ENDNOTES

1. Joseph Henry Thayer, *Thayer's Greek Lexicon* (1889).

2. "Ambassadors of the United States," Wikipedia, last revised October 31, 2024, accessed November 6, 2024, https://en.wikipedia.org/wiki/Ambassadors_of_the_ United States.

3. Emma Dibdin, "6 Podcasts About Lies, Scams and Con Artists," *The New York Times*, December 19, 2023, updated January 3, 2024, accessed January 3, 2024, https://www.nytimes.com/2023/12/19/arts/podcastsscams-con-artists.html.

4. European Union, "AI can write a new Bible," *CNE.news*, June 6, 2023, accessed November 6, 2024, https://cne.news/article/3207-ai-can-write-anew-bible.

5. Josh McDowell, *Evidence That Demands A Verdict, Volume. I: Historical Evidences for the Christian Faith* (Great Britain: Campus Crusade for Christ, 1972), 175.

6. "What Was the Pre-Flood Population Like?," Answers in Genesis, January 6, 2016, accessed November 6, 2024, https://answersingenesis.org/noahs-ark/pre-floodpopulation/.

7. "What does the Bible say about holiness?," Got Questions Ministries, last updated January 4, 2022, https://www.gotquestions.org/holiness-Bible.html.

8. Jessica Stillman, "New Princeton Research: People Judge Your Competence Based on Your Clothes in Under 1 Second," Inc.com, December 19, 2019, accessed November 6, 2024, https://www.

inc.com/jessica-stillman/newprinceton-research-people-judge-your-competencebased-on-your-clothes-in-unde-1-second.html.

9. Jessica Van Roekel, "A Prayer for Continuous Joy – Your Daily Prayer – May 1," WWTC 1280 AM/FM 107.5 The Patriot, accessed November 6, 2024, https://am1280thepatriot.com/devotionals/yourdaily-prayer/a-prayer-for-continuous-joy.

10. Deirdre Clemente, "Why and When Did Americans Begin To Dress So Casually?," *Time*, August 5, 2015, accessed November 6, 2024, https://time.com/3984690/american-casualdressing/.

11. Scott Raines, "Perspective: The dressing down of America," *Deseret News*, April 30, 2023, accessed November 7, 2024, https://www.deseret.com/2023/4/30/23691348/johnfetterman-sweats-clothes-dressing-down-goblinmode-ralph-laure/.

12. Peggy Noonan, "The Senator's Shorts and America's Decline," *The Wall Street Journal*, September 21, 2023, accessed November 7, 2024, https://peggynoonan.com/the-senators-shorts-andamericas-decline/.

13. "Adm. McRaven Urges Graduates to Find Courage to Change the World," *UT News*, May 16, 2014, last updated November 8, 2024, accessed November 8, 2024, https://news.utexas.edu/2014/05/16/mcravenurges-graduates-to-find-courage-to-change-theworld/.

14. Jim Lucas, "What is the second law of thermodynamics?," Live Science, February 7, 2022, accessed November 9, 2024, https://www.livescience.com/50941-second-lawthermodynamics.html.

15. Albert Barnes, *Barnes Notes on the Bible* (1830s).

16. Robert Jamieson, Andrew Robert Fausset, and David Brown, *Jamieson-Fausset-Brown Bible Commentary* (1871).

17. John Gill, *Gill's Exposition of the Entire Bible* (1746 and 1748).

ENDNOTES

18. James Strong, *Strong's Exhaustive Concordance of the Bible* (Iowa Falls, IA: Riverside Book and Bible House).

19. Sacha Pfeiffer, "Disgusted by city's top prosecutor, a police officer refuses to testify, NPR, November 23, 2023, accessed November 9, 2024, https://www.npr.org/2023/11/23/1214894247/disgusted-by-citys-top-prosecutor-a-police-officer-refusesto-testify.

20. L. E. Maxwell, *Born Crucified* (Chicago, IL: Moody Press, 1945), 86-87.

21. Paul Brownback, *The Danger of Self-Love: Reexamining A Popular Myth* (Chicago, IL: Moody Press, 1982), 14-15.

22. *Quality-Adjusted Life Years and the Devaluation of Life with Disability*, National Council on Disability, November 6, 2019, accessed November 9, 2024, https://www.ncd.gov/assets/uploads/reports/2019/nc d_quality_adjusted_life_report_508.pdf.

23. Sherry Palmer, "Fatherless Single Mother Homes Statistics," Fix Family Courts, March 20, 2017, last modified July 19, 2023, accessed November 9, 2024, https://www.fixfamilycourts.com/divorcechild-custody-blog/single-mother-home-statistics/.

24. Paul Hemez and Chanell Washington, "Number of Children Living Only With Their Mothers Has Doubled in Past 50 Years," United States Census Bureau, April 12, 2021, accessed November 9, 2024, https://www.census.gov/library/stories/2021/04/number-of-children-living-only-with-their-mothers-hasdoubled-in-past-50-years.html.

25. Sarah Javaid and Jasmine Tucker, "National Snapshot: Poverty Among Women & Families, 2021," National Women's Law Center, September 2021, accessed November 9, 2024, https://nwlc.org/wpcontent/uploads/2021/11/NationalSnapshotFS1.pdf.

26. "Legalism (theology)," Wikipedia, accessed November 9, 2024, https://en.wikipedia.org/wiki/Legalism_(theology).

27. Gone with the Wind, directed by Victor Fleming (1939; Beverly Hills, CA: Metro-Goldwyn-Mayer).

28. Post readers, "Bowman's vulgar, profane political rally: Letters to the Editor — June 25, 2024," *New York Post*, June 24, 2024, accessed November 9, 2024, https://nypost.com/2024/06/24/opinion/repjamaal-bowmans-vulgar-profane-political-rallyletters/.

29. "Jewish Concepts: The Name of God," Jewish Virtual Library, accessed November 9, 2024, https://www.jewishvirtuallibrary.org/the-name-ofgod.

30. Avery Blank, "4 Ways Successful People Use Their Name To Gain Respect," Forbes, July 10, 2018, accessed November 9, 2024, https://www.forbes.com/sites/averyblank/2018/07/10/4-ways-successful-people-use-their-name-to-gainrespect/.

31. Erwin W. Lutzer, *God's Devil* (Chicago, IL: Moody Publishers, 1996), 43.

32. "Scribe," Wikipedia, accessed November 9, 2024, https://en.wikipedia.org/wiki/Scribe.

33. George L. Kelling and James Q. Wilson, "Broken Windows," *The Atlantic*, March Issue 1982, accessed November 9, 2024, https://www.theatlantic.com/magazine/archive/1982/03/broken-windows/304465/.

34. "What is the meaning of the foxes in Song of Solomon 2:15?," Got Questions Ministries, accessed November 9, 2024, https://www.gotquestions.org/foxes-SongSolomon.html.

35. *Oxford English Dictionary*, established 1857.

ENDNOTES

36. "The False Hope of Purgatory," *The Master's University*, accessed November 9, 2024, https://www.masters.edu/thinking_blog/the-falsehope-of-purgatory/.

37. "What does the Bible say about Purgatory?" Got Questions Ministries, accessed November 9, 2024, https://www.gotquestions.org/purgatory.html.

38. Don Piper, *90 Minutes in Heaven: A True Story of Death and Life* (Grand Rapids, MI: Baker Publishing Group, 2004), 25.

39. Piers Steel, "The art of keeping up with yesterday," *The Globe and Mail*, March 11, 2011, accessed November 9, 2024, https://www.theglobeandmail.com/opinion/the-artof-keeping-up-with-yesterday/article4266163/.

40. "How Many People Die Each Day in 2024?," World Population Review, accessed November 9, 2024, https://worldpopulationreview.com/countries/deaths-per-day.

41. Valerie Strauss and Daniel Southerland, Washington Post, "HOW MANY DIED? NEW EVIDENCE SUGGESTS FAR HIGHER NUMBERS FOR THE VICTIMS OF MAO ZEDONG'S ERA," *The Washington Post*, July 16, 1994, accessed November 9, 2024, https://www.washingtonpost.com/archive/politics/1 994/07/17/how-many-died-new-evidence-suggestsfar-higher-numbers-for-the-victims-of-maozedongs-era/01044df5-03dd-49f4-a453a033c-5287bce/.

42. Meg Sullivan, "UCLA demographer produces best estimate yet of Cambodia's death toll under Pol Pot," UCLA, April 6, 2015, accessed November 9, 2024, https://newsroom.ucla.edu/releases/uclademographer-produces-best-estimate-yet-of cambodias-death-toll-under-pol-pot.

43. r/explainlikei'mfive, "ELI5: Why is it that during loud concerts you feel the bass in your chest but not the higher notes despite them being the same volume.," Reddit, accessed November 9, 2024, https://www.reddit.com/r/explainlikeimfive/comments/wyny47/eli5_why_is_it_that_during_loud_concerts_you_feel/?rdt=40554.

44. Tia Ghose, "The Human Brain's Memory Could Store The Entire Internet," *Live Science*, February 18, 2016, accessed November 9, 2024, https://www.livescience.com/53751-brain-couldstore-internet.html.

45. John Angell James, *The Anxious Inquirer After Salvation* (London: The Religious Tract Society, Instituted 1799), 1-2, 56, 65, 164.

46. L. E. Maxwell, *Crowded to Christ* (Chicago, IL: Moody Press, 1976), 11-12.

47. Krista Tippett, "Living the Questions," On Being, October 20, 2022, accessed November 9, 2024, https://onbeing.org/programs/living-the-questions/.

48. "Eternal Security," Accessed May 12, 2025, https://en.wikipedia.org/wiki/Eternal_security.

49. The Editors of Encyclopedia Britannica, "Pascal's Wager," *Encyclopedia Britannica*, December 13, 2022, accessed November 9, 2024, https://www.britannica.com/topic/Pascals-wager.

50. James Strong, *Strong's Exhaustive Concordance of the Bible* (Iowa Falls, IA: Riverside Book and Bible House).

51. Robert Wimer, "A Galilean Wedding," robertwimer.com, June 12, 2022, accessed November 9, 2024, https://robertwimer.com/agalilean-wedding/.

ENDNOTES

52. Randy Alcorn, "What Are the New Jerusalem's Dimensions?," eternal perspective ministries, February 22, 2010, accessed November 9, 2024, https://www.epm.org/resources/2010/Feb/22/whatare-new-jerusalems-dimensions/.

53. Erin McDowell, "25 of the most expensive celebrity memorabilia items sold at auction," *Business Insider*, updated May 18, 2020, accessed November 11, 2024, https://www.businessinsider.com/mostexpensive-celebrity-memorabilia-items-sold-atauction?op=1.

54. Adrian F. Ward, "Scientists Probe Human Nature-and Discover We Are Good, After All," *Scientific American*, November 20, 2012, accessed November 9, 2024, https://www.scientificamerican.com/article/scientists-probe-human-nature-and-discover-we-are-goodafter-all.

55. "Compromise," *Collins Dictionary*, https://www.collinsdictionary.com/dictionary/englis h/compromise/related#:~:text=workable%20compro mise-,A%20compromise%20is%20a%20situation%20in%20which%20people%20accept%20something,%5 B...%5D&text=If%20you%20accept%20something %20that,%5B...%5D.

About the Author

Garry Harris is a former minister, retired USPS Letter Carrier, and now a retired Realtor. At 57, he married the love of his life, Wanda, and in that moment became a husband, father to Kristen and Chad, and grandfather of two. Since then, Garry has been blessed with four more grandchildren. He and his family now reside in the Kansas City area.

Contact Info:
flashesandwhispers@gmail.com

www.ingramcontent.com/pod-product-compliance
Lightning Source LLC
Chambersburg PA
CBHW072155070526
44585CB00015B/1156